*Illustrated Cornucopia
of Arts and Crafts Techniques:*

*A Media Approach
for the Elementary Teacher*

Illustrated Cornucopia of Arts and Crafts Techniques:

Parker Publishing Company

A Media Approach
for the Elementary Teacher

Gretchen S. Sanderson

West Nyack, N.Y.

Illustrated Cornucopia
of Arts and Crafts Techniques:
A Media Approach
for the Elementary Teacher
by Gretchen S. Sanderson

© 1979 *by*

PARKER PUBLISHING COMPANY, INC.

West Nyack, N.Y.

Library of Congress Cataloging in Publication Data

Sanderson, Gretchen S
   Illustrated cornucopia of arts and crafts techniques.

   Includes index.
   1. Art--Study and teaching (Elementary)
2. Activity programs in education. I. Title.
N350.S28   372.5'044   78-10933
ISBN 0-13-450841-6

Printed in the United States of America

This book is dedicated to my little artists—
Kenneth, Mark, Erik and Courtney.

Introduction

Elementary teachers are constantly seeking new ideas to use in motivating students, and many have found art or craft projects valuable. They often develop creative approaches to the curriculum by integrating art or craft lessons into lessons in English, geography, history or social studies. To do this effectively, teachers need to become familiar with many tools and media used by arts and crafts people. Once a teacher familiarizes herself with many techniques and ideas, and the characteristics of many materials, she can apply these to what she knows about the skills, imagination, ability levels, understanding, and performance of her pupils.

The objective of this book is to stimulate learning about different tools, materials, ideas and techniques used in arts and crafts through some enjoyable projects in which each of them is used.

The first part consists of nine chapters, each containing five lessons in which the potentials of various art techniques are discussed and demonstrated. In each lesson the use of correct tools, the methods, and anticipated results are described. For example, a teacher might note the characteristics of acrylics, which are strikingly different from other paint media—their brilliant colors, rapid drying, permanency, and textural effects.

A good way to get acquainted with any artistic medium, old or new, is to produce something in it on a small scale. The teacher can approach each chapter by considering a relatively simple application, and then use this as a gauge for further projects, based on the size of her class, the working area available, subject matter related to the medium, and the ability levels of her children.

The second part of this book offers you ideas related to various crafts, describing projects ranging from easy-to-construct small items to more complicated articles, including a number of projects that may be carried over two or three lesson periods, depending upon ability level and time available. Here the discoveries pupils have made about media in Part One may be applied to specific craft works, and you will see when to use various techniques, where and how to use them, and when to transfer skills from one medium to another.

Throughout both parts you will be shown ways to stimulate the imaginations of your pupils, encouraging each one to investigate, discover, and explore his own individuality, ability for self-expression, and capacity for artistic enjoyment. The book is written in anticipation that elementary teachers will find it a ready reference and practical, stimulating guide.

Gretchen S. Sanderson

Table of Contents

*Illustrated Cornucopia
of Arts and Crafts Techniques:*

*A Media Approach
for the Elementary Teacher*

COLOR CHART

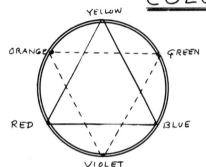

PRIMARY COLORS   YELLOW - BLUE - RED

SECONDARY COLORS   ORANGE - GREEN - VIOLET

TERTIARY COLORS   MADE BY MIXING THE SECONDARY COLORS

ORANGE and GREEN   =   CITRINE
ORANGE and VIOLET   =   RUSSET
GREEN and VIOLET   =   OLIVE

INTERMEDIATE COLORS

YELLOW ORANGE – YELLOW GREEN – BLUE GREEN
BLUE VIOLET – · RED VIOLET – RED ORANGE

VALUES

WHITE   LIGHT GREY   MIDDLE GREY   DARK GREY   BLACK

TINTS =   MADE BY ADDING WHITE TO COLORS
SHADES   MADE BY ADDING BLACK TO COLORS

COMPLEMENTARY COLORS

YELLOW OPPOSITE VIOLET
ORANGE OPPOSITE BLUE
GREEN OPPOSITE RED

ANALOGOUS COLORS
ARE NEIGBORING COLORS

YELLOW, GREEN, BLUE   OR
YELLOW GREEN, GREEN, BLUE GREEN
(ANY ADJACENT COLORS)

Color Chart

16

chapter one

Multiple Ways to Use
Colorful <u>Crayons</u>

The popular crayon becomes an exciting tool when all its potentials are explored. Crayon activities can range from those of early childhood into work at the high school level. To get the best results from crayons, boys and girls should make certain preparations. A pad of newspapers under the drawing will form a cushion, resulting in brighter colors and softer, blended strokes. Once you have selected a set of newspaper pads, save them for your crayon lessons, storing them flat on a shelf the rest of the time.

There are various styles of crayons: large ones, small ones, semi-flat, square, crayons of water-soluble color, wash-away color, and crayons for drawing on fabric. An appealing feature of crayons is that every bit can be utilized in different techniques. This chapter describes ways of holding crayons, and the effects created, as well as alphabet cartoons, open and contour stencils, triple crayon drawing, crayon resist, crayon and heat, rubbed crayon, drawing with melted crayon, crayon etching, paper batik using crayon, and other techniques.

lesson 1

Four Hand Positions

Procedure:

There are four basic ways to hold crayons. The first and second positions are illustrated in Fig. 1-1A. The first way is the natural writing position, in which a pupil can produce fine lines in any direction. The second is an inverted position, in which the crayon is held vertical while it is twisted and pressed down. Have your boys and girls experiment with this method, then have them slant the crayon at an angle to use the edge of the crayon base for fine lines, an alternate way to use the crayon when the point becomes dull.

The third and fourth ways (Fig. 1-1B) require that you remove the wrapper of a broken crayon and use the side. Try pushing the crayon away from you with even pressure on the total crayon; this produces one even tone, while putting pressure on one end results in a graded tone. A helpful suggestion is to collect broken crayons just for your class experiments with broad stroke techniques. If your pupils start with dark colors first, they'll see instant results. The fourth method is to cut notches on the side of the crayon. Odd numbers make interesting designs, as you will see when you pull the crayon toward you. Next try twisting the crayon to right and left without lifting off the paper, then

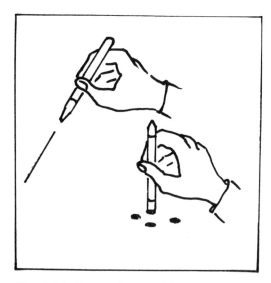

Fig. 1-1A: First and second hand positions.

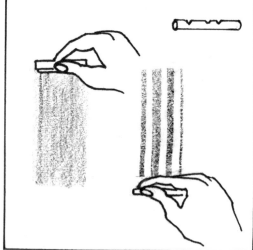

Fig. 1-1B: Third and fourth hand positions.

try a geometric pattern, a wavy motion, a spiral; all kinds of hand movements create interesting results.

Have your boys and girls combine these techniques in a weed composition with pussy willows and grasses (Fig. 1-1C). They may also try a bowl with twisted buds (Fig. 1-1D). Have them use the pointed end to draw an alphabet letter "A," for example, and, using their imaginations, develop it into a head (Fig. 1-1E). In another example, using the letter "D" creates the nose and upper face (Fig. 1-1F). Added hair is made with the side of the crayon.

Fig. 1-1C: Weed composition.

Fig. 1-1D: Twisted buds and vase.

Fig. 1-1E: Letter "A" cartoon.

Fig. 1-1F: Letter "D" cartoon.

lesson 2

Open and Contour Stencils

Procedure:

Cut two pieces of cardboard exactly the same size. A four-inch square is an easy proportion to handle. With pencil draw a flower shape in the center, then go over the line with a black marker to clarify the cutting. A simple way to cut out the flower and retain smooth edges is to start at the outside edge of the cardboard and cut to the black flower outline (Fig. 1-2A). After the flower falls out, tape the cut edges together on both sides.

Take the second cardboard and find the center by drawing lines from corner to corner, creating an "X." The intersection is the exact center. Place a coin over this spot (a penny is a good size) and draw around it. Proceed to cut out the center in the same manner as you did the first cardboard (Fig. 1-2B).

Fig. 1-2A: Cutting the first open stencil.

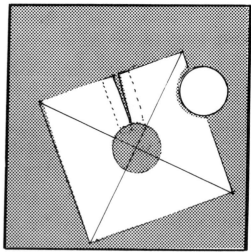

Fig. 1-2B: Cutting the second open stencil.

Now you have four stencils, two ''open'' and two ''contour,'' for making designs on paper.

An excellent inexpensive paper is the financial section of the newspaper, for it offers a greyed, textured background. Place the *open* stencil (the square cardboard with the flower cut out) on the newspaper and draw around the four-inch square. This outline of the cardboard is a necessary guideline for the following stencil.

Holding the stencil firmly in place begin drawing, with a bright color, lines from the cardboard onto the newspaper, continuing all around the opening. Lift off the stencil and enjoy the dramatic sunburst effect. Next place the second *open* stencil with the small penny cut out exactly over the first one and fill in the center with a darker color. Remove (Fig. 1-2C).

If you use the *contour* stencils (the solid flower and penny shapes), you produce totally different designs. Place the contour flower stencil on white or colored drawing paper and draw lines from the cardboard off onto the white paper, all around the shape. Do the same with the penny contour stencil but use a different color crayon. This creates a new style of flower (Fig. 1-2D).

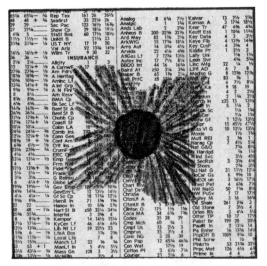

Fig. 1-2C: Open stencil on newspaper.

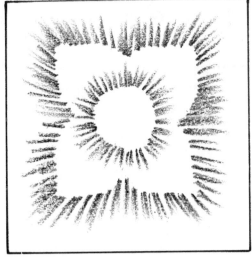

Fig. 1-2D: Contour stencil on white paper.

lesson 3

Triple Crayon Strokes

Procedure:

Select three contrasting colored crayons; place them flat on the table and tape them together, being sure the points are in line with each other. Next tape three colors in a cluster group, again having the points lined up. Draw with the flat ones and tap or stipple with the cluster (Fig 1-3A). Experiment with a variety of hand and arm motions—spiral, circular, angular; draw hills, trees, letters, numbers, and again the plant life motif (Fig. 1-3B).

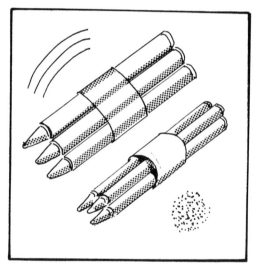

Fig. 1-3A: Triple crayon, flat and cluster.

Fig. 1-3B: Triple crayon both ways.

lesson 4

Crayon Resist

Procedure:

A most unusual effect and a constant surprise to pupils is produced by the crayon resist method, especially "white on white" pictures. It consists of drawing with a white crayon on white paper. First have each girl and boy plan a theme in pencil, then go over the lines with a black crayon or marker. In this instance, a snow scene was planned. Simply place this drawing under the white paper and follow the lines with white crayon. Next, a watercolor wash was prepared of a fairly strong grey color, and starting at the top of the drawing a full brush of the grey watercolor was brushed over the whole drawing. As the wash flowed over the wax crayon it ran off those areas but was absorbed into the uncovered paper. A snowstorm can develop, to the surprise and pleasure of the pupils (Fig. 1-4A).

Fig. 1-4A: White crayon on white paper crayon resist.

lesson 5

Crayon, Heat and
Wax Paper

Procedure:

The best approach to this technique is through experimentation, without having your class plan any subject matter or discuss how it is to be used. It is essential to prepare a working area first by covering your table with a thick layer of newspapers. On this place a sheet of wax paper and have class members sprinkle bits and shavings of bright colored crayons, moving them apart from each other to allow space for the colors to run and overlap a little. Place a second sheet of wax paper over the crayon particles (Fig. 1-5A).

Next, heat a household iron to warm temperature and press down on the wax paper and crayon bits (Fig. 1-5B). The crayon will melt and run. Move the

Fig. 1-5A: Crayon shavings between wax paper.

iron around until the whole paper is heated, applying the heat only until the desired effect is obtained; then unplug the iron. The wax paper cools off instantly so it can be handled in different positions to find the color combinations and design that appeal to the class. In this case, a fish was cut out to be used as part of a mobile (Fig. 1-5C).

Almost any subject can be used and designs for any season can be made, using appropriate colors. This technique is excellent for window transparencies.

Fig. 1-5B: Pressing and melting the crayon bits between wax paper.

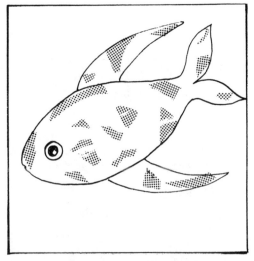

Fig. 1-5C: Fish cut out of pressed wax paper.

lesson 6

Crayon Rubbings

Procedure:

Crayon rubbings are always a delightful activity, interesting everyone from young children to adults. Your class will need bits of paper, so have scrap paper in your classroom to select shapes from, or cut original abstract forms. There are many ways to experiment with rubbings, but to illustrate a contrast, collect an odd number of shapes and place them between two sheets of easel paper. The inexpensive easel paper is ideal for this purpose. Using the side of a crayon, pull it down over the scraps, revealing the pattern; be sure to hold the papers securely at the top with your other hand. The result is dark-edged shapes with a middle tone all over the background (Fig. 1-6A).

To illustrate another effect, simply overlap the paper shapes and proceed as before (Fig. 1-6B). These colorful sheets can be used on the bulletin board to mount spelling or math papers, lending them a little art atmosphere.

Does the group of shapes suggest a picture? With colored markers draw a picture over this background, incorporating the shapes. Try large shapes on 18″ × 24″ paper.

Fig. 1-6A: Separate scraps.

Fig. 1-6B: Overlapping scraps.

lesson 7

Melted Crayon Drawings

Procedure:

Drawing or painting with melted crayon or wax is an ancient art technique called encaustic, or "burning in." This lesson is ideal for a small group of older children interested in exploring a new method. Since an open flame is used, close, careful supervision by the teacher is vital. Foil or asbestos sheet should be on the table and a candle well secured in a tin can.

First, have the pupil make a drawing, keeping in mind simplicity, directness and texture. In this case, a horse's head was drawn in profile and the strokes pre-planned. Select the colors and begin. Place the crayon in the flame and apply to the drawing, continuing to stroke with the crayon after the melted wax has been deposited. This gives two kinds of texture to the finished work (Fig. 1-7A). Immediate application of the crayon from the flame to the drawing is essential as the melting process lasts only a fraction of a minute.

Another application is a study of a flower basket using white and black crayons on grey paper. Here the white petals were melted on first, then the black centers (Fig. 1-7B). To preserve these drawings, a clear-drying liquid called Mod Podge was painted over the entire surface of each sketch. When applied, it looks like milk but dries clear.

Fig. 1-7A: Horse's head in melted crayon. Fig. 1-7B: Basket and flowers on grey paper.

lesson 8

Crayon Etchings

Procedure:

It is best to have your pupils keep etchings on a small scale, due to the amount of crayon needed to cover the paper and the etching process itself. To create this moonlight theme only two crayons were used, black and white. Draw a four-inch square on white paper, leaving at least an inch of margin, since your drawing will need trimming. Cover the area with white crayon, first vertically and then horizontally. Next apply a coat of black crayon in both directions. Have your sketch in front of you for easy viewing, and proceed to etch out the drawing, using a knitting needle, a toothpick, or any tool that leaves a clear white line. The moonlight scene is a good beginning picture (Fig. 1-8A). A sunset, in which the under colors are worked out and applied, then covered, can be equally striking.

Another method of applying bright colors is to make abstract patches of bright and lighter colors, omitting purple and brown, leaving black for the final covering.

Fig. 1-8A: Moonlight theme, etched crayon.

lesson 9

Crayon Paper Batik

Procedure:

Batik is a dyeing method in which parts of a fabric are covered with removable wax. The designed fabric is crushed before being dipped into a dye, letting the dye seep into the cracks. You can produce a type of "batik" on paper, using all colors of crayons and watercolor washes. It is wise to begin with a drawing on white paper in black crayon. After practice, your class can try colors and washes.

In this example, the subject was drawn, then the paper was submerged in a pan of water and crushed in both hands. It was opened and re-crushed, to break the surface and give the drawing the batik look. A watercolor wash was then applied with a brush over the entire drawing, and where the broken surface of the paper occurred the watercolor dye clung to the cracks. Keep subject matter simple and not too detailed (Fig. 1-9A). The finished work can be ironed flat or left naturally rumpled. Here again is a technique enjoyed by all, from the early grades to the upper levels, especially since every result is different. The crushing of the paper alone has a certain appeal for the pupils.

Fig. 1-9A: Crayon paper batik.

lesson 10

Wash-Away Crayons

Wash-away crayons are packed in a small box of four colors—red, blue, green and brown. Although these crayons are primarily designed for marking Texaprint plastic papers, charts and globes, they can be used successfully on white, smooth finished paper plates. This is an extra budget saver for it provides practice until a final picture is decided upon and gives the pupil a new and different experience.

Procedure:

Have each boy and girl draw a landscape or still life on a paper plate. Have them study their drawings, think how they can be improved, then with a wet sponge simply wipe them off to begin again (Fig. 1-10A). There is no need for water at the table because a damp sponge will last a long time.

In this example, this pumpkin still life was washed off six times, leaving the plate in good condition for further work. However, when a drawing is to the child's liking, tack it up on the bulletin board. You can arrange a group of drawings in a pleasing design, such as plates in a circle, a square, a rectangle, or simply in a row.

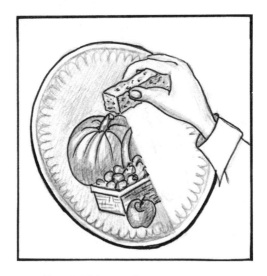

Fig. 1-10A: Wash-away crayons.

lesson 11

Watercolor Crayons

In a box of watercolor crayons, there are 12 two-inch long color crayons, each having a black cardboard collar to protect the fingers while working, since these crayons are water soluble and easily transfer colors to the fingers.

Procedure:

There are two approaches in using the crayon, and both are exciting. Start off with a newspaper pad under the drawing paper and make a ½″ margin all around the sides. Tape this paper at the corners to the newspaper pad to prevent it from curling forward, which happens when one side is dry and the other wet. Brush with clean water and a brush, cover the entire surface to the margins, then select a dark crayon for contrast and scribble freely over the wet surface. Your pupils will enjoy watching the colors spread and crawl in fascinating action. Turn the crayon upside down on the flat end and move it around creating wide dark strokes (Fig 1-11A). If the paper begins to dry, simply drop water over it; do not brush it on, as brush strokes will wash some of the color away. Set this paper aside to dry; then, turning it in different positions, try to find images that you can color.

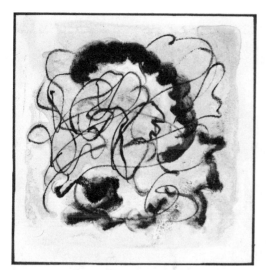

Fig. 1-11A: Watercolor crayons applied to totally wet surface.

Fig. 1-11B: Watercolor crayons applied to spots of wet surface.

A good exercise in imagination is to "see" birds and animals in the wet shapes and color them appropriately. On another sheet of white paper, apply spots of water—some large, some small, leaving a good part of the paper dry. In the wet areas scribble with watercolor crayons to make flower forms. Then draw the stems on the dry paper, making sharp clear lines, adding leaves, small buds, and some other shapes of flowers (Fig. 1-11B).

To experiment with many colors, have the class draw patches side by side of bright reds, yellows, greens, but this time they will brush over all of the patches with a wet brush. Notice how the colors run together, resulting in a muddy, brown "all-over" tone. This may be ideal in some pictures, but if, for example, you want a bright autumn foliage picture, keep the colors separate by wetting only one color at a time, and while wet, working more color into that area.

lesson 12

Fabric Crayons

Fabric crayons are boxed in eight colors with directions for their use on the back cover. However, you should know that these can make colorful drawings on cloth. Fabric crayon designs become permanent on a piece of cloth when pressed with a hot iron. The result is machine washable but should not be put in the dryer or cleaned with bleach.

Fig. 1-12A: Central balance design on paper.

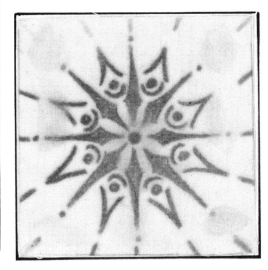

Fig. 1-12B: Central balance.

Procedure:

An easy way to begin a design on cloth is with a single shape such as a circle, square, diamond, etc. Then branch out from the center, drawing more details, to produce a design with central balance. You might draw different shapes on the blackboard to motivate the children or start with a discussion pointing out shapes in the room. Encourage the pupils to create their own shapes and color combinations on white paper, keeping each one separate for contrast. Begin with a small four-inch square, placing a shape like a circle in the center; then extend slender diamond shapes, adding half moons between them; continue with darts and dots (Fig. 1-12A).

When the design has been colored, it is ready for transfer to cloth with a hot iron. Use of a synthetic fabric insures permanency, but old cotton sheeting is excellent for most purposes. Prepare the work table with a pad of newspaper on top of which is placed white drawing paper, then the fabric, next the colored design, face down, and another piece of paper on top, so the iron is not directly over the design. Press with a hot iron at cotton temperature until the image begins to appear. Remove the paper pattern and the crayon image will have been transferred to the fabric (Fig. 1-12B).

The paper transfer cannot be really used again unless re-colored, but you may want to try it for your own information. You'll see that only a light image results. Instead of discarding the paper patterns, which are fairly bright, you might mark off squares on colored construction paper and mount these, showing a small amount of background color between. The whole class can be represented in a wall hanging made up of many all-over designs (Fig. 1-12C).

Fig. 1-12C: Wall design made from the designs of 16 pupils.

Monograms with Fabric Crayons

Pupils in upper grades will want to try creating their own monograms of two or three letters well related to each other. One important element to be considered in working with letters and numbers is that they must be prepared in reverse. First design the monogram, then place it up against a window in reverse and trace it so it appears backwards (Fig. 1-12D). Color this in one or two colors. Follow the procedure for transferring, resulting in a permanent individual design (Fig. 1-12E). Numerous gifts can be made—tote bags, neckties, shirts, aprons, etc.

Fig. 1-12D: Monogram reversed.

Fig. 1-12E: Monogram transferred to fabric; correct position.

lesson 13

Crayon Montage

Procedure:

The crayon montage consists of a single clipping from a magazine pasted onto a sheet of drawing paper on which the pupil draws in a suitable background. A simple way to plan for this almost self-motivated lesson is for the teacher to collect, ahead of time, a box of torn-out pages from magazines, depicting subjects her class is interested in. Waiting until lesson time to hand the children magazines in which to find their pictures is too distracting; it is human nature to become absorbed in advertisements and stories. After each child has selected his picture, suggest that he concentrate on making a background for it. An easy subject matter is the boy and his balloons (Fig. 1-13A). The young artist will easily think of adding such details as clouds, a hill, a fence and three balloons. Given the picture of a cat, you may lead pupils to see how a fish tank can be added, with lines in white drawn over the cat to make it look as though he is in back of the fish tank (Fig. 1-13B).

It is easier to color the background if you place your magazine clipping on a definite spot on the paper, then trace around it. You can then set it aside until you have completed the background. As a final step, glue the clipping in place. School paste dries and cracks and is apt to make the clipping "bubble." Use water soluble glue instead.

Encourage older pupils to try more pictures, organizing the clipping and background so they are equally strong in color and composition. Older boys and girls can use these montages as ideas for original stories and poems.

Fig. 1-13A: Crayon montage used as background for clipping.

Fig. 1-13B: Variation on a theme: cat in back of fish tank.

chapter two

Fingerpainting Activities for Tactile Fun

Fingerpainting offers a wide range of art expression for everyone from small children to adults. It is a fallacy to think that this art should be practiced by kindergarten children only, since it can be enjoyed at all age levels. Fingerpainting produces a freedom of self-expression, confidence, and composition through hand and arm movement that pencils and crayons can't equal. Older children will find this a medium for storytelling through the fingers and a tactile experience they can thoroughly enjoy. Among adults, fingerpainting may be traced to its Oriental origins. Centuries ago Chinese artists literally used their fingers and fingernails dipped in paint to create pictures of exquisite beauty; in fact, fingernails were often grown long as an important tool in this distinctive art. We still look to Chinese and Japanese fingerpainting artists for inspiration and instructional value, studying the delicacy of their interpretation of nature.

The first American artist to introduce fingerpainting in our schools was Mildred Shaw. She developed a heavy creamy paint which was spread on surfaces with the fingers and hands, rather than brushes. She first created this technique in an American school in Italy to give children more artistic freedom and a completely different experience from that of pencils and crayons. She brought this fresh new outlook to America where she taught teachers how to use this medium in their classes. It became a popular art lesson and an exciting adventure for everyone.

In this chapter we will not plunge into the usual large-scale activity of fingerpaint with huge sheets of paper, plentiful fingerpaint and many colors. Rather we will first work with this technique on a small scale to get the feel of the paint, the hand positions, the preparation of paper and the preparation of hands for easy cleanup. There is a simple way to make cleaning hands after fingerpainting easy. Before each session, pour some dish detergent into the palms of your hands and rub your hands together thoroughly, putting detergent even under the fingernails and around the cuticles. Let it dry; it is pleasant on the hands. Then begin the lesson, and when you have finished, simply wash your hands in warm water. The protective coat of detergent will make suds and clean your hands quickly. This same method can be used for cleaning off other media as well.

Materials:

(The materials listed here are used throughout Chapter 2.) Fingerpaint; fingerpaint paper; baking pan, wide enough for width of paper; large container for extra water; rags or paper towels; newspapers, smock or man's shirt worn backwards; plastic spoon; dishwashing liquid; gesso; fixative and tools for unusual effects.

Fingerpaint Substitutes:

1. Mix wallpaper paste as directed on package; spoon onto wet paper and add dry powdered paint or poster paint; spread over paper with hand.
2. Cornstarch fingerpaint is made by boiling paint colors with one quart of water and ½-cup cornstarch. First dissolve cornstarch in small amount of cold water and slowly add boiling water. Let it cook until it becomes thick, adding dry powdered paint or poster paint. Mixtures of this nature tend to sour after a while so add a few drops of oil of wintergreen as a preservative.
3. Spray liquid starch onto wet fingerpaint paper or wet the paper with bottled liquid starch, then add poster paint.
4. Place a small amount of school paste in center of a wet paper and add poster paint; mix together with flat of hand.

Fingerpaint Paper Substitutes:

1. Use brown wrapping paper or cut open a large brown grocery bag. Smooth the paper with a damp sponge until free from wrinkles and paint one coat of gesso over the entire surface. Use a 2"-wide house brush. Have the strokes neatly applied in one direction. When dry it is ready for fingerpainting. Wash brush.
2. Foil is an excellent substitute, although care in handling it is essential, since foil tears more quickly than wrapping paper. When the design is fingerpainted on foil, reflective strokes are seen, adding sparkle to the picture. The foil should be lightly taped to the work surface to prevent slipping.

3. Spraying white drawing paper with fixative prevents the surface from absorbing too fast, thus making it a fairly good fingerpaint paper.

4. Light-colored Con-Tact paper, plain or with a faint design, can be used with interesting results. A major advantage is that it can be mounted without paste. Merely peel off the backing and adhere it to a colored background.

5. Brightly colored magazine pages can also be used. Do not work too long on this surface or the paper becomes limp and the picture dulled. Discuss the idea first. When the young artist starts with a definite idea that relates or contrasts with the magazine page theme, he can add his painting quickly and directly, without constant changes.

6. Wallpaper with a soft design has a strong surface similar to fingerpaint paper and is another good challenge for creative ideas. Wallpaper stores frequently have old books of samples that they will give away to art classes, and these sample books can be used for many other art projects as well.

lesson 1

Discovering and Experimenting

Objectives:

To encourage the child to invent ways of obtaining effects without the restriction of directed goals.

Procedure:

Wet the fingerpaint paper by dipping it into the pan of water, slowly pulling it through so both sides are wet. Place it on the table, gently smoothing out wrinkles; start at the center with both hands flat on the paper and move outward. Place a small amount of fingerpaint in the center and fold the paper in half; slowly open and let it dry. A double design will result (Fig. 2-1A). Try folding the paper the opposite way before opening; four partial shapes will result.

The next step produces all sorts of fantasies in landscape themes and undersea motifs. Place the paint on the wet paper, and holding the hands stiff and flat create a smooth background. Be sure there is enough paint and that it is not too thin; then place a second sheet over the first, rub gently and pull off. The action of pulling draws the paint to one side resulting in three-dimensional effects that have the appearance of mountains, valleys and rocks (Fig. 2-1B).

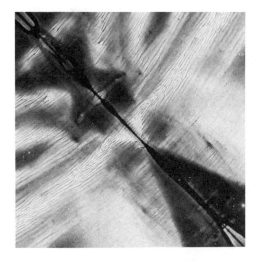

Fig. 2-1A: Double design.

Fig. 2-1B: Three-dimensional painting.

Again prepare the background of color, fairly strong and smooth. Keep the background tone fairly even; then crush a tissue into a soft ball and press firmly into the paint. Repeat, occasionally turning tissue to a clean side. All kinds of imaginative animated figures appear (Fig 2-1C). Later this technique can be used on larger paper with bigger wads of crushed tissue for effects of trees in full foliage, jumbo flowers, clouds, etc.

Finally, if you are teaching older boys and girls, try creating an "antique" background. With flat hands produce an even tone; next try spotted

Fig. 2-1C: Animated figures.

Fig. 2-1D: Antique effect.

effects; then simply pick the paper up and crush it with both hands—do not twist it, just crush it into a large ball. Open the ball gently, and stretch it out. Do not smooth the paper with your hands or the pattern will be spoiled. Let the paper dry (Fig. 2-1D), then iron it on the wrong side on brown wrapping paper. The result is a crackled design like old paper, ideal as a background for colored cutouts, collages, or even for large block letters for P.T.A. meetings or posters, plays, announcements, etc.

Fingerpainted paper can also be used to cover books, provided it is varnished. After a fingerpainting has been ironed and is flat, apply varnish as a protective coat. This is an excellent technique that appeals to older pupils, even in junior high school.

lesson 2

Results of Hand Positions

Objectives:

To introduce the basic use of the thumb, fingernails and hand.

Procedure:

The background should be even in tone and as free from patterns as possible, since the fingernails will create a smaller line. Hold the fingers in a drooping position like an inverted flower bud; keeping this hand in a "frozen" pose move the total hand in a circular motion, watching the continuous spiral circles appear. These circles make excellent flowers, or weeds, and you can add grasses and stems. Just turn your palm upward and brush the fingernails on and off the paper (Fig. 2-2A).

The thumb alone creates beautiful broad strokes. Prepare the paper with a fairly solid tone, and holding your thumb stiffly on its side, proceed to make sweeping motions in the shape of the letter "n." Any time the thumb is stopped the paint collects and produces a dark accent. You can either lift it off and let it dry or proceed to practice this striking effect (Fig. 2-2B). This stroke is ideal for ruffled collars for clown heads, waves in the ocean, big clouds, etc.

Combine these two techniques for dramatic flowers; apply the thumb stroke first and then the fine fingernail accents (Fig. 2-2C).

To develop a series of bands, use the side of your hand. Due to the short finger and the inundations of the bones and muscles, the side of your hand is a natural tool. As the paint is moved along by your hand, it collects, making dark areas (Fig. 2-2D). The dark bands can be used for cutout letters in poster making, and when held vertically, the striped surface appears to resemble

Fig. 2-2A: Fingernail flowers.

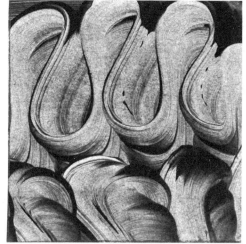

Fig. 2-2B: Thumb strokes.

Fig. 2-2C: Dramatic effects.

stalks and grasses. Let your imagination develop other ideas as you turn the paper around for different angles.

Prepare your background again but this time, holding the side of your hand stiff, start at the lower left of your paper and zig-zag your hand up and down, fanning out the design until a palm leaf motif is obtained. This is a popular stroke in fingerpainting (Fig. 2-2E). The shapes you produce can be cut out and arranged into a collage, making a striking composition on contrasting colored paper.

Fig. 2-2D: Fingerpaint bands.

Fig. 2-2E: Palm leaf.

lesson 3

Using Different Tools

Objectives:

While painting with fingers is the primary method of using this type of paint, discovering what effects different tools make with fingerpaint is worth the experience.

Procedure:

Before your lesson, prepare a number of short narrow strips of light-weight cardboard about ¼″ wide. Coat fingerpaint paper with an even tone; then, using one of the cardboard strips, pull lines down in a wavy fashion, exposing the clean white ¼″-lines. First practice the waves (Fig. 2-3A). Then move the cardboard strips in different directions, overlapping, meeting, and finally drawing pictures.

Cut another piece of cardboard, but this time cut your own original shapes at one end (Fig. 2-3B). This shows the shape of the cardboard that created the

Fig. 2-3A: Waves, using cardboard strip.

Fig. 2-3B: Shape of cardboard tool.

Fig. 2-3C: Design made with cardboard tool.

geometric and curved design for Fig. 2-3C. By experimenting with the cardboard contour, you find ways to add texture to a picture where it is needed—for bricks, bark, shingles, etc.

Try using the cutout in a circular design. Make a white dot on the wet fingerpaint paper by lifting a speck off. Keep your eye on this white center and work around it with the cut cardboard, moving it toward the center and out in a fan shape, continuing until the circumference has been completed (Fig 2-3D).

The small comb is always interesting to work with. You'll find a series of fine lines results when the comb pushes the paint aside. Try one wide sweep in an arch shape, in which you twist a bottle cap in place, creating open circles (Fig. 2-3E). Once these have been used, you can add fingerpaint techniques with the side of your hand or your thumb to enrich your design.

Old toothbrushes make soft fine lines, and pressing a sponge into the paint produces multiple holes impossible to imitate (Fig. 2-3F). A series of these tool techniques can be made during a splashy fingerpaint day. Then, when these dry, in another lesson you can cut them out and assemble them to form a very unusual three-dimensional picture.

Most classrooms have old rulers that can be also used as fingerpaint tools, producing still another effect. Hold the ruler on the wet paper and simply press down and twist, keeping it flat on the paper. Lift off and repeat (Fig. 2-3G). Try the experiment of sliding the ruler around without lifting it off the paper.

Fig. 2-3D: Central design, using cardboard tool.

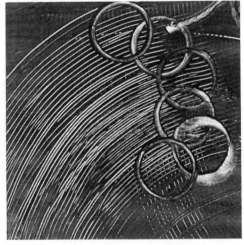

Fig. 2-3E: Ring effect.

Fig. 2-3F: Design using toothbrush.

Fig. 2-3G: Design using ruler.

lesson 4

Experimenting with Printing Techniques

Objectives:

Combining old and new ideas with fingerpaint, show the class how to save a picture and then continue painting and making multiple prints. This can be fascinating even at the junior and senior high school level.

Procedure:

Frequently the first try at making a picture with fingerpaint is very successful, and it seems discouraging to have to wipe it out in order to continue painting. A simple way to make a copy of the picture and at the same time add the charm of texture is to gently place a sheet of paper toweling over the fingerpaint and with both hands press over the entire picture. Lift the towel off by picking it up at the top corners, and place it on a newspaper to dry. You now have a copy with the rough texture of the towel added (Fig. 2-4A).

To make a monoprint, plan a simple cutout flower or an animal motif. Two blossoms and two leaves are used here (Fig. 2-4B). Mount this arrangement on a piece of cardboard. Rub fingerpaint gently over the entire cardboard,

Fig. 2-4A: Paper towel print.

Fig. 2-4B: Cutout cardboard "printer."

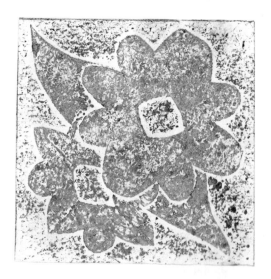

Fig. 2-4C: Print from cutout.

both the cutout figures and the background. Place a sheet of white paper over it. This sheet need not be fingerpaint paper; white drawing paper will do. Press and rub, being sure the entire cutout and the background receive the pressure. Lift off and let dry. This can be repeated for several prints (Fig. 2-4C).

Rubbed designs are not confined to crayon and chalk; rubbing is very effective with fingerpaint. Using the same motif can serve as further practice. Place a wet sheet of fingerpaint paper on top of the mounted cutout and apply fingerpaint. Rub gently over the surface, feeling the edges of the mounted flowers, watching them come into focus (Fig. 2-4D).

Pulled string is a popular experiment, and endlessly exciting because no two prints are ever alike. Holding a 12″-piece of string in the left hand, poke all but the last two inches of it into the fingerpaint. *Do not let go of the last two inches.* To remove the excess paint, simply hold two fingers of your right hand on the string and guide the paint off down the length of the string. If you are righthanded, transfer the string to your right hand and place a sheet of white paper on the newspaper. Dangle the string over the paper, and slowly, in circular motions, lower it until a spiral pattern rests on the paper, leaving a long stem of string that hangs off the paper by two inches. Place another sheet over the wet string, then a magazine on top of that. Let your left hand spread out on top of the magazine. With your right hand pull the two inches of leftover string out slowly and with even pressure (Fig. 2-4E). Lift off both the magazine and the top paper to find a beautiful calla lily in a pulled string technique.

For the older level, try sewing thread; this creates a fine delicate flower. Try three lilies on the same paper, letting each one dry before proceeding to the next one, and experimenting with different colors.

Fig. 2-4D: Fingerpaint rubbing over cutout.

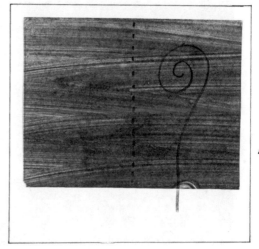

Fig. 2-4E: Pulled string technique.

To make a dual print, fold the white paper and follow the directions given above, but plan the flower on one half; when finished, two lilies in reverse prints will appear (Fig. 2-4F). Cut out and mount.

Finger monograms are fun. Each child can make his own initials mounted on colored paper for display at a P.T.A. meeting (Fig. 2-4G).

Small greeting cards are easy to make, using fingers, toothpicks, the end of a pencil or cut cardboard (Fig. 2-4H).

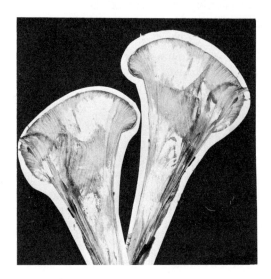

Fig. 2-4F: Reversed prints.

Fig. 2-4G: Monogram.

Fig. 2-4H: Greeting card design.

lesson 5

Scrap Pictures

Objectives:

Left-over scraps offer a challenge to the imagination. Many beautiful strokes and textures are found in these pieces, which through creative inventiveness can become unusual and dramatic pictures. Only a light application of paste is needed for mounting.

Procedure:

The study of American Indian culture can lead to wigwam pictures made of fingerpaint scraps. Many pieces can be cut in tent shapes, incorporating designs from leftovers (Fig. 2-5A). These can be arranged in sizes from large to small, giving depth to a picture. Start with large ones in the foreground and put progressively smaller ones in the distance. When the pupils have worked in color, save the scraps in a community box and share in making these colorful Indian pictures.

Boats are always a favorite with children, and here is another opportunity to select colored and black and white scraps for the boats, sails and watery effects (Fig. 2-5B).

Fig. 2-5A: Fingerpaint wigwams.

Fig. 2-5B: Fingerpaint sailboats.

Another boat can be made of Con-Tact paper. This is good since it removes the problem of paste. Simply cut out the boat, sails and waves, and secure in place (Fig. 2-5C).

Boys will enjoy cutting out trucks of all shapes and sizes, selecting their scraps carefully to make interesting types of trucks with a variety of lines and shadings (Fig. 2-5D).

Fig. 2-5C: Con-Tact paper sailboat.

Fig. 2-5D: Fingerpaint truck.

Buildings in shadow and airplanes are also popular and easy to cut out. Detail can be added to the scrap by using crayons and markers. Many children will find this vital to complete their picture (Fig. 2-5E).

Flowers are a natural theme for scrap fingerpaint pictures. The daffodil (Fig. 2-5F) is a good example of how three dimensional a blossom can appear through selection of shaded scraps.

Fig. 2-5E: Fingerpaint plane.   Fig. 2-5F: Fingerpaint daffodil.

chapter three

Coloring with Vivid Cray-Pas and Soft-Toned Payons

Introduction to Cray-Pas

Cray-Pas are a mixture of crayon and pastel, non-toxic, non-waxy, with extremely brilliant hues. A box of 12 includes three primary colors (red, yellow, blue), two secondary colors (orange, green), plus white, grey, brown, and black (violet is not included). These colors can be heavily applied, sketched lightly, or rubbed on with your finger or cloth for smooth blending. Cray-Pas are not recommended for very young artists, or for any work in large areas. Due to the softness of Cray-Pas, they wear away rapidly so are too expensive for such use. More mature pupils, however, will find working with them an exciting experience since few crayons yield such vivid colors, and Cray-Pas offer opportunities for detailed and broad etching techniques.

At whatever age level you introduce this medium, plan to confine your projects to those with small areas, which will reveal all the characteristics needed to understand Cray-Pas.

If your objective in a picture is to make use of bright, clean, colors, don't drag one color into the other. The sticky quality of Cray-Pas makes it pick up other hues, easily depositing bits of color in unwanted places. You should, however, practice mixing and pulling colors into each other on a sheet of scrap paper to see for yourself what happens. For some subjects, streaked and dulled colors are desirable. When any work is finished with Cray-Pas, spray it with a fixative such as Krylon to prevent smudging when pasting and mounting.

lesson 1

Blending Colors

Procedure:

Practice drawing a leaf form in two contrasting colors, leaving a narrow space between them; then repeat this, but this time blend the colors together, either with your finger or a cloth (Fig. 3-1A). Use this same technique in drawing a fish and notice how rounded and three dimensional the body appears (Fig. 3-1B).

Fig. 3-1A: Blending colors.

Fig. 3-1B: Fish with blended colors.

lesson 2

Reverse Etching

Procedure:

Every teacher knows the value of motivation before a lesson, to encourage and develop inspiration and enthusiasm. Before this lesson, display large clear photographs in the classroom, especially pictures having textures, such as animals, fish, birds, bark, foliage, etc. For the etching in this example, a bird was selected. First the bird was drawn lightly with a pencil, then with a pad of newspaper placed under the drawing and with the use of a dull-pointed instrument such as a knitting needle, all the lines were redrawn, using enough pressure to indent the surface of the paper without breaking through it. The side of the Cray-Pas was then rubbed over the entire drawing, after which the strokes were blended by rubbing over it again with a cloth wrapped around the finger. Notice how the indented lines remain white (Fig. 3-2A). Some lines may receive more Cray-Pas than others, but this only adds to the charm of the picture.

Fig. 3-2A: Reverse etching bird.

lesson 3

Wax Paper Etching (Drawing Paper Saver)

Procedure:

Tape a sheet of white drawing paper with a sheet of wax paper on top of it to the newspaper pad, then rub a darker color over almost the entire surface, leaving some areas free from Cray-Pas. Rub the entire wax paper with a cloth, so that the part free from Cray-Pas will only have a light tone, adding a varied background of values instead of the usual solid tone. A dull-pointed knitting needle is an excellent tool. Select the width of line you want by practicing first; the smaller the needle, the narrower the line. A #8 needle is easy to hold and yields a good line. An ocean theme was used here to etch out the rocks, sea and lighthouse (Fig. 3-3A). Mount on white paper to accent the etched lines. This is a good lesson to ease the classroom budget and save on white drawing paper. (A package of 12″-wide wax paper contains about 41 yards.)

Fig. 3-3A: Wax paper etching lighthouse.

lesson 4

Abstract Rubbed Background

Procedure:

Treating the background separately before imposing the design adds a three-dimensional effect. This can be done successfully in tones of grey and white as well as full color. For example, shades of blue in light tones make an ideal background for bright yellows and orange blossoms with dark centers. Another reason to encourage the production of abstract rubbed backgrounds is that this technique develops individual expression as no two pictures will be alike. Sometimes the direction of the strokes can suggest a theme; vertical and swaying lines might remind the pupil of a landscape of grasses with a farmhouse for center interest, or horizontal rubbings might suggest a seascape. A theme of weeds, grasses and flowers is seen in Fig. 3-4A. The white Cray-Pas was pressed down and lifted off, depositing more of the crayon by the heavier application. This makes a pleasing contrast of background and foreground subject matter.

Fig. 3-4A: Abstract rubbed background,
flowers superimposed.

lesson 5

Cray-Pas 3-D Collage

Procedure:

Because of the unusual brilliance of Cray-Pas and the popularity of the subject matter, fruits were chosen for this lesson. Be sure the newspaper pad is under the white drawing paper. Draw all the fruits separately from each other, beginning first with light pencil sketches. Then color in the fruits with bright color—the pear, for example, a bright yellow with the edges shaded with orange to create a rounded effect. When all the fruits have been colored cut them out; never cut before coloring or the edges will be torn easily.

A pear, an apple and a plum were selected for this lesson, to be mounted in three-dimensional style, creating supports of masking tape to hold the fruit away from the background paper. Roll an inch of masking tape, sticky side facing out, and wrap it around a pencil (Fig. 3-5A). Slip it off and set aside on wax paper while two others are made. Turn the pear face down on wax paper and center the masking tape support by inserting the pencil again and applying pressure (Fig. 3-5B). Do the same with the two remaining fruits. Plan to have the fruits overlapping for a pleasing arrangement. The pear was pressed down first, then the apple, and last the plum—which overlaps the pear since it is in front. These raised fruits will create a shadow on the background paper resulting in a three-dimensional collage (Fig. 3-5C).

Fig. 3-5A: Preparing for 3-D collage.

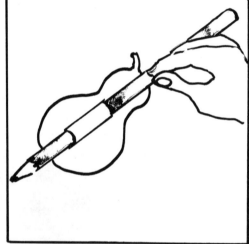

Fig. 3-5B: Securing cylinder to back of cutout pear.

Fig. 3-5C: Completed 3-D Cray-Pas collage.

lesson 6

Textured Cray-Pas

Procedure:

This lesson is an exercise in developing textures, using one color; later, color combinations can be explored. All these textures can be drawn on one sheet of 9″ × 12″ white drawing paper with a black Cray-Pas or any dark color.

A simple beginning is the small dot pattern, also called stippling. Since the Cray-Pas is soft, noisy tapping isn't necessary; merely press down, lift off and the Cray-Pas immediately responds. On another part of the paper use the Cray-Pas upside down; press the crayon down, twist, turn, and a large dark dot results. Use a broken piece to rub a stroke on its side, creating a broken tone or wood-grained look. Try a fan-shaped design, very dark, with irregular edges, and finally begin with a dark value and end with a light tone; rub these together to create a gradation from dark to light.

Cut out these five textures into five different shapes using realistic, geometric or freeform shapes, then arrange them to make a pleasing composition, balancing the darks and lights (Fig. 3-6A).

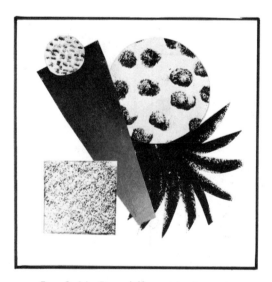

Fig. 3-6A: Five different textures in
abstract shapes.

lesson 7

Two-Tone Etching

Procedure:

This is a study where only two Cray-Pas are used—black and white on grey paper, making a two-tone etching. Again select a subject with strong texture. In this case a sugar maple tree was drawn against a grass-covered hill with cumulus clouds overhead. Color in the white cumulus clouds first and proceed to lay a grey tone over the rest of the picture. Blend the strokes together with a cloth wrapped around the fingertip. Determine the contour of the hill and with black Cray-Pas draw it in. Color the lower half of the scene all black over the grey. Continue to draw the tree into the sky, tapering the branches into a lace-like pattern against the grey sky. With the etching tool, etch lines in the bark and branches and grass, keeping in mind that the grass nearest the lower edge of the drawing will be taller and thicker, and as it recedes will become shorter and closer together (Fig. 3-7A).

For a complete contrast to this lesson try a landscape in autumn with brilliant bursts of colorful foliage. Plan these autumn scenes so they abut, being sure to make each hill join the next one for a continuous border.

Fig. 3-7A: Two-tone etching.

Introduction to Payons

Payons is a coined word meaning "painting crayons." These produce crayon drawings which can be finished like a watercolor. Payons are packed eight to a box—red, yellow, blue, green, orange, violet, black and brown, but no white. Each Payon has a black protective collar because of the water soluble consistency of the medium. Payons are one of the most economical art tools and are good budget savers since there is no waste at all; even the smallest crumb can be dissolved into a watercolor wash. Cleaning the hands after this lesson can be a quick process if, as suggested before, dish detergent is poured into the palms, worked into the skin and allowed to dry before starting the lesson. Rinsing the hands afterward instantly removes the color.

Another practical value of the collar is that it makes it possible to use broken Payons easily by simply wrapping a piece of masking tape around the end of the Payon and inserting into the collar until it is firmly in place (Fig. 3-8A).

Fig. 3-8A: Using a collar to hold broken Payon.

lesson 8

Wet and Dry Technique

Procedure:

Again work in a small area to learn the potentials of the medium. Wet an area with water, using the #7 watercolor brush found in most watercolor boxes; immediately draw into it with your chosen colored Payon. Watch the pigment become active, crawling and spreading out in all directions.

In another part of the paper place spots of water; then begin drawing a line on the dry paper, passing through the wet spots and onto the dry paper again. See how the character of the line changes. This can be very useful in creating pictures and designs (Fig. 3-8B).

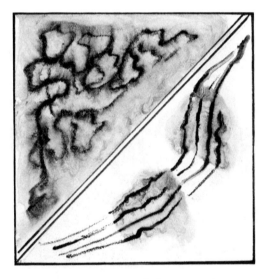

Fig. 3-8B: Wet and dry examples.

lesson 9

Payon Paper Mask

Procedure:

A sheet of 9″ × 12″ white drawing paper, or even a colored sheet, is ideal for a full face mask. Just shape the lower part in an oval contour; do not cut it out until all the Payon work is done. Draw around the total mask with a bold line, adding colored ones for decoration. Include your own imaginative designs to increase the dramatic quality of the mask. Finally dip the paint brush in water, paint over all the lines, and watch the colors spring into brilliant hues (Fig. 3-9A). When dry, cut the mask to fit the face, tie strings to top corners, and it is ready to wear. Try a cloth mask, but be sure the fabric is taped down for easy drawing.

Fig. 3-9A: Paper mask exaggerated.

lesson 10

The Side of the Payon

Procedure:

When the protective collar is removed, naturally more color will be transferred to the fingers, so the dish detergent solution on the hands preceding the lesson will prove beneficial. Paint a wash of clean water (but not too much water) over an area of about five inches, then with the side of the Payon make sweeping curved lines like big leaves (Fig. 3-10A). With the end of the Payon, make dots for accent.

Fig. 3-10A: The side of the Payon creates
striking moths.

lesson 11

Portrait Painting

Procedure:

Watercolor washes are made instantly with Payons by stirring with the Payon stick just long enough to dissolve the pigment. Grey is used here for reproduction purposes, but the red and yellow combined make a fine flesh tone. Begin with a lightly penciled portrait of a boy, then wash a tone over the entire head, neck and shoulders (Fig. 3-11A). While the wash is slightly damp, draw in the hair and features. The shirt can be drawn in when dry, however. Experiment until you have control over the wetness of the wash and the reaction of Payon strokes. (See Fig. 3-11B).

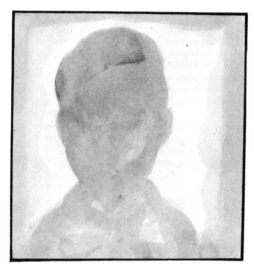

Fig. 3-11A: First step in portrait—Payon wash.

Fig. 3-11B: Second step in portrait—accents added.

lesson 12

Masking Tape Exercise

Procedure:

The use of masking tape to retain white areas while painting a wash can be extremely useful. A good way to become acquainted with the method is to work in abstract shapes first; just tear or cut different sizes of tape and apply them to white drawing paper in a small area. Mix a fairly strong wash and cover the entire area (Fig. 3-12A). Let it dry and peel off the tape; clean white areas result. Think how these forms, now abstract, can become realistic shapes—boats, animals, and endless other ideas.

Fig. 3-12A: Masking tape abstracts.

lesson 13

Masking Tape Landscape

Procedure:

Plan a landscape lightly in pencil—house, trees, clouds, foreground. Pre-plan where the direction of sunlight is coming from, then cut and shape pieces of masking tape to represent the white areas, securing them to the drawing (Fig. 3-13A). When dry, peel off the tapes and complete the picture with Payons, wet and dry. Add water with brush strokes and re-apply Payons for richer, darker accents (Fig. 3-13B).

Fig. 3-13A: First step in landscape—using masking tape.

Fig. 3-13B: Masking tape landscape finished.

lesson 14

Sponge-Printing with Payons

Procedure:

A boat theme would be an interesting subject for this lesson. Mix a strong wash of blue by stirring the blue Payon in water until it is the brightness you want. Plan the drawing on white paper—a sailboat and low horizon; then dip the dampened sponge into the blue wash and press down over the top of the picture, sail and boat, but not below the horizon. With the sponge turn it on the corner and drag horizontal strokes across the paper, leaving white areas for sparkle and white caps. While the background sponged sky is damp, draw over the outline of the sails and boat; possibly add a brush full of water over the boat and redraw it with the Payon for more depth and richness. (See Fig. 3-14A.)

Practice with the sponge technique for unusual effects; even try cutting sponges into various shapes and print these in overlapping designs.

Fig. 3-14A: Sponge-printed sky.

chapter four

Easy-Flowing Tempera Experiments

Introduction

Tempera paint is a universal medium, employed by nearly all artists. It has been in existence for many years, used not only throughout the school systems, but an avid favorite among commercial artists as well. In early Latin and Italian writings, the word *tempera* meant any liquid medium to which pigments were added to produce paint. Later the word was restricted to pigments combined with egg yolk. Presently it includes all painting techniques that employ emulsions. Emulsion is a stable aqueous (watery) liquid with an oil, fatty, wax, or resinous substance. (Reference: *The Artist's Handbook* by Ralph Meyer, published by the Viking Press, New York, 1940.)

Tempera is the direct opposite of watercolor—definitely an opaque medium to which white paint is frequently added. Tempera paint dries to a matte (dull) finish, is non-toxic, and will not rub off. The manufacturers of the paint have made it available in numerous colors, boxes, jars, tubes, and even markers. For easy reference, several types are listed here:

- Tempera "cakes" of six colors, each set in a durable plastic caddy, which can be stacked while wet, are a great asset for the busy classroom teacher.
- A box of 16 brilliant, semi-moist colors is excellent for an older group.
- A still larger size, called "Biggies" (two inches square and a half-inch thick), come in 24 colors arranged in a plastic tray.
- Tempera may also be purchased in convenient pint or quart sizes, in unbreakable squeeze plastic bottles with spouts for easy dispensing. There are also 12-ounce, see-through plastic dispensers with attached

caps. The advantage of this container is that you can keep it capped, which means that the paint will not collect and harden in the spout, so a constant flow of paint is assured.

- There is a new tempera called "Non-drip," which comes in nine colors, never needs stirring, and is packaged in wide-mouth containers.
- Gold and silver tempera is available for seasonal decorations.
- Sets of black, white and grey paints, including five cool greys and five warm greys, with no mixing to bother with, are helpful to mature art classes in their study of values.
- The "Tempera Marker" involves no dripping, no spilling, no brushes; yields wide strokes; comes in six colors—red, yellow, blue, green, black and white.
- A different form of tempera is dry powder paint, which is water soluble, odorless, non-toxic, smooth when mixed with water, and prepared in 16 colors, plus gold and silver.
- For detailed and small color accents, tempera can be purchased inexpensively in a cardboard slide box of six jars, two inches tall, with plastic caps. The colors are red, yellow, blue, green, black and white.
- Also very helpful are four mixing media: a thinner to dilute paint (optional); liquid for textiles for permanency and washability; a medium added for silk screening and fingerpaint; a medium added to prepare tempera paint for block printing.

Experiment, explore and investigate this wide range of tempera paints for your particular art projects, and use the suggestions in this chapter to develop your skills, interest and enthusiasm in the wonderful world of tempera.

lesson 1

Wash-Away Tempera Pictures

Procedure:

The wash-away technique is exciting, surprising, unusual, and distinctive. For economical reasons it is best to practice on 4″ × 6″ white paper, and even the finished work need not be larger than 9″ × 12″. It is essential that the subject be simple, preferably in profile, with an easily recognizable contour,

In the center of the paper draw a fish, also add a ½″ margin around the edge of the paper. This keeps the paper flat; otherwise, if painted to the edges it will curl under. With white tempera paint fill in the fish outline; let it dry.

Brush black paint over the entire area within the border; it does not have to dry completely to proceed with the technique.

The purpose of this activity is to wash away bits of black paint by holding the paper under a stream of cold water from the faucet. It won't take long to learn that too forceful a stream of water will ruin the effect. The black flakes off due to the smooth white coat of paint underneath, and the result is an interesting textural effect on the fish where bits of paint remain (Fig. 4-A). Later explore with pastel colors for the subject and a dark color for the top layer.

Fig. 4-1A: Wash-away tempera—fish motif.

lesson 2

Counterchange (Black and White or Two Colors)

Procedure:

Counter means "opposite," and change implies a different position. This is another economical lesson since only one color is used; the other color is the white paper. Again cut a 4″ × 6″ size for practice, using your own initials for the first experiment. A ½″ border has advantages: it creates a fingerhold when the paper is wet and prevents curling under. With pencil divide the area in half and draw large block type letters, positioning them on the paper so that they are also cut in half (Fig. 4-2A). Paint the left side solid black, except for the letters, which remain white; on the right side paint the letters only.

The most important element of counterchange is the transition from black to white; the structure must remain consistent, with no change of shape (Fig. 4-2B). This counterchange is a bold, powerful style of art seen on billboards, posters, and especially in advertising art. Encourage the pupils to look for examples. Once this theory is understood try a curved, swirling black design. Keep both subject and background simple for best results.

Fig. 4-2A: Counterchange letters outlined—
first step.

Fig. 4-2B: Counterchange letters painted—
second step.

Plan in pencil a boat against a swirling line (Fig. 4-2C). Now paint the left half of the swirl black. The part of the boat that enters the black area remains white. Conversely, the part that enters the white background will be painted black (Fig. 4-2D). The boat must retain its clear-cut shape.

Fig. 4-2C: Swirling background and boat motif.

Fig. 4-2D: Counterchange—boat and swirling background painted.

lesson 3

Crushed Tempera

Procedure:

Mix a strong color of middle value, halfway between black and white, on small paper while practicing. Paint the entire area with a solid wash (Fig. 4-3A). While the paper is still wet, pick it up and crush it with both hands into a ball (Fig. 4-3B); open it to dry. When all moisture has disappeared place it on a pad of newspaper and iron it flat. A handsome crackled effect is produced, due to the fact that the paint has been quickly absorbed by the broken surface of the paper. This unusual textural paper is ideal for letters, such as P.T.A. posters. Animals in silhouette also can be used in collage work (Fig. 4-3C).

Fig. 4-3A: Solid wash background for crushed tempera.

Fig. 4-3B: Crushing paper with wet wash.

Fig. 4-3C: Letters and squirrel cut out of crushed, dried and ironed tempera wash.

lesson 4

Dripping Imaginative Pictures

Procedure:

There are two techniques in the dripping method—one for wet and one for dry paper. In the wet process brush clear water over the entire area, again leaving a dry margin. Have a puddle of strong dark color in the palette into which the brush is dipped until it is full and dripping, then immediately brush it under the top margin, repeating a few more strokes. Hold the paper up a little from the table to allow the paint to flow downward, even tipping it sideways for different directions. Replace it on the table to dry so some of the white paper is left for contrast (Fig. 4-4A).

Now try dripping the wet paint on dry paper, starting with a few horizontal brush strokes. Hold the paper up and individual streams of paint will flow down. Let it dry flat. Turn it upside down to discover a suggested landscape, with trees in the foreground. These only need added branches and some animals, perhaps a few deer (Fig. 4-4B).

Fig. 4-4A: Dripping technique on wet paper.

Fig. 4-4B: Dripping technique on dry paper, with dry subjects added.

Explore another wet technique and let the result spark your imagination; perhaps you will discover the shape of a dog (Fig. 4-4C). The only additional stroke added to this drip picture was the upper leg; all else was due to tipping the paper at different angles.

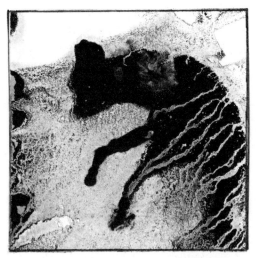

Fig. 4-4C: Picture of dog that resulted from dripping technique.

lesson 5

Producing a
Central Balance Design

Procedure:

One of the most beautiful examples of central balance design is found in churches. Called a rose window, and usually made of stained glass, it consists of shapes radiating out from the center. Another simple example of central design is a clock. Many examples can be displayed in the classroom illustrating this principle: flowers (looking into the blossom), jewelry, and certain dinner plate designs. Encourage the students to find central balance designs in magazines at home and bring them to class. A good size to work with is made by simply taking a 9″ × 12″ paper and marking it into a 9″ × 9″ square; the left-over strip can be the color-testing paper. To find the center, essential in this design, draw lines from corner to corner; where they cross is the exact center

(Fig. 4-5A). This design grows from the center outward, using a variety of shapes.

Motivate the lesson by a class discussion of objects in the room that are in the shape of circles, ovals, triangles, and various other forms. Since this design grows from the center, a framework of four branches would be helpful to build on. Sketch the design, continuing until the square is filled. Later, with an older group, try purely free brush work, inventing and creating interesting original shapes with a definite color scheme. These will be individual, creative growing designs well worth displaying.

Fig. 4-5A: Four steps in growing design.

lesson 6

Newspaper Blot Shapes

Procedure:

Blot experiments with tempera paint on newspaper can develop unusually fascinating shapes. Newsprint or newspaper is ideal for this work because of its absorption quality. Fold a small piece of newsprint or newspaper in half; open and place a blot of paint, any color, on the fold, one in the center, above and below; then fold the paper, rubbing it evenly with the hands. Open to reveal an equally balanced shape (Fig. 4-6A). This shape was cut out and mounted on white paper for contrast.

Use three values or colors in the next experiment. Mix three puddles, black, grey and white; paint dabs of white paint first, then grey and finally black, folding the paper for a different design. Open and outline the shape created with a dark brush line, adding small dots for accents (Fig. 4-6B). Try white paint on black paper: fold it, open flat and add lines following the contours and dots. This will be a strikingly attractive blot design (Fig. 4-6C).

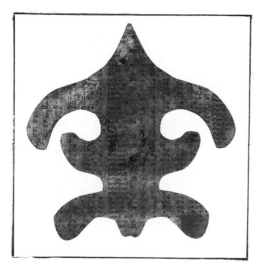

Fig. 4-6A: Formal balance design made from blots of paint on folded newspaper.

Fig. 4-6B: Blot design in black, grey and white with outlines and accents of dots.

Fig. 4-6C: White blot on black paper with free brush additions.

lesson 7

Sgraffito and
Dry-Brush Tempera

Procedure:

In sgraffito, you scratch away paint; "sgraffito" means scratching. In dry brush you remove paint with a brush. Be sure your pupils practice these techniques before trying any picture-making, to establish their self-confidence. Sketch a house on a hill in pencil and prepare a puddle of black or dark paint, using one color to begin with (this allows more concentration on the technique than realism in color). Paint the dark area of sky first; then turn the brush upside down, using the pointed wooden end, or use any instrument that will cut through the paint—a long nail, sharp plastic fork, etc.—and draw vertical lines to simulate trees in the distance.

Dry brush takes a little more patience, but once you master the technique, you and your pupils will enjoy the results. Make a fairly thick puddle, of more paint than water. Hold the brush firmly in your hand, and without changing your grip dip it into the puddle and simply drag it upward on the paper, in the direction grass grows, until a series of fine hairlines appear. Leave the part of the hill nearest the house all white (Fig. 4-7A).

**Fig. 4-7A: Tempera sgraffito and dry brush
landscape.**

lesson 8

Funny Face with One Finger

Procedure:

This is a fun lesson, especially for the lower grades. For the first funny faces no brush is needed, only one finger. (For these pictures, the middle one was used.) Dip your finger in paint and onto the paper for the first eye; dip your finger again for the second eye; use only a light touch for the end of the nose. The mouth is made in two strokes—from the left corner to the center and from the right corner to meet the first stroke (Fig. 4-8A). Repeat faces over the paper, leaving enough space around each one to keep them distinct (Fig. 4-8B).

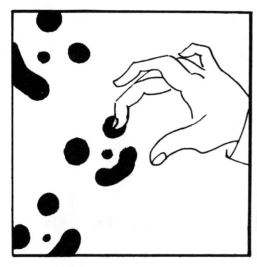

Fig. 4-8A: Funny finger face application.

Fig. 4-8B: Allover pattern of finger funny faces.

Experiment with one large face, this time adding, with a brush, hair, pupils, eyebrows, ears, neck and shirt (Fig. 4-8C). The class will produce a variety of expressions, positions and hair styles. These heads could be cut out, mounted on sticks and used to act out talking parts of a play.

Fig. 4-8C: One large funny face with free
brush additions.

lesson 9

Newspaper Brush Prints

Procedure:

Newspaper can be used for tempera paint where thin washes are not required. You and your pupils will come to enjoy newspaper as a painting background. Prepare three bright and strong colors for a flower theme. Press the brush into the lightest color and simply place it, tip first, near the center of the paper, pressing the rest of the brush down to create an oval shape. Repeat this in a circle, making petals; do not let them touch each other. Continue with other flowers in different colors, making a total of odd numbers; five is a good number. For the centers, drop a small wet puddle of contrasting color and immediately pull out radiation lines with the wooden or plastic end of the paint brush. Do this to all the centers, making some with dark centers and some with light (Fig. 4-9A).

Another popular subject is the pussywillow. The stem can be drawn first, or the pussywillows themselves in grey paint. While wet add the white paint to the top and black to the base for the cups that hold the florets. Finally add the stem with dark brush strokes, completing the composition with long curved grasses (Fig. 4-9B).

Fig. 4-9A: Black-grey-white brush prints for flower motifs on newspaper.

Fig. 4-9B: Pussywillow brush prints and grasses in black, white, grey on newspaper.

lesson 10

Clipping Tempera Pictures

Procedure:

This project challenges children to use their imaginations to create an original background for a selected magazine clipping. The young artist does not have to draw a center of interest; the clipping serves that purpose. However, it takes thought to plan a good composition and a harmonious background for the subject. It's best not to pass out magazines to the class, since the distractions of stories, pictures and advertising will dampen any enthusiasm for the project. Instead, the prepared teacher will have a box of appropriate clippings (torn out of magazines) that suit the age level of her class. Animals are favorites. The deer shown here (Fig. 4-10A) were carefully cut out (without antlers, which were drawn in later). Next, the cutout was placed in various areas of the paper before the pupil decided on a final spot. The deer were then traced around and the background was painted. The last step was to glue the clipping in place.

A popular theme, especially with the boys, would be motorcycles; girls might also select this theme. Think of localities that make interesting backgrounds for this rider (Fig. 4-10B). A country road with strong sunlight making dramatic shadows is effective.

Fig. 4-10A: Magazine clipping mounted on tempera background inspired by the clipping.

Fig. 4-10B: Motorcycle figure in strong sunlight on road.

chapter five

Using Transparent Watercolor's Fluid Play

Introduction

Transparent watercolor is a distinctive medium in which no white paint is added. (If white is included, the medium no longer is transparent but is opaque, a "heavier" technique given the name *gouache*.) Watercolorists who call themselves purists prefer to use fluid watercolor in which the white paper is their greatest asset, shining through the thin wash. Oftentimes the white paper is left dry in some areas to create brilliance and contrast.

Elementary School Watercolor

Watercolor sets suitable for use by elementary school children are manufactured in eight or 16 colors. Boxes are made up with dry pigment placed in half-pans. In the eight-color box the basic colors are red, orange, yellow, green, blue, violet, brown and black, in that order. White is not included, but this is excellent for transparent watercolor work. The box usually contains a number seven brush, and the cover has three recessed sections for mixing paint. If larger washes are needed, plastic containers are helpful, leaving the cover palette for smaller mixes.

The first step at any level, but especially in grade school classes, is to prepare the work table for the watercolor lesson. Time spent on this will result in freedom in painting, protection of table, and an aid in cleanup. Spread newspaper over the area and tell each pupil to arrange his or her equipment on the right side of the table—for right-handed children. Left-handed pupils may prefer theirs on the left side. Each child should open the watercolor box with the cover nearest him or her. Remove the brush; cut pieces of white paper, for color testing; and put out a tissue for unexpected brush surplus. Select a water container that has a wide mouth and that is heavy enough so it won't tip over. Too small a tin can means the pupil will have to change water continuously. The more water a can can hold, the longer it will take to darken from the pigments. The final item is white paper; regular drawing paper is fine for grade-school girls and boys.

If watercolor washes are painted to the edge of the paper, it will contract and curl under. To prevent this have your class simply draw, either freehand or with a ruler, a ½" margin on the four sides of the paper. This dry border will keep the paper flat. It is none too early to teach the children as many ideas as possible to make watercolor painting enjoyable without discouraging features.

As the final step before actual painting and while discussion concerning the lesson is finishing, have pupils place a few drops of water on the dry paint in each half-pan of color. A few minutes' wait allows the paint to absorb the moisture, making the colors readily accessible. Otherwise the pupils often force the brush into the dry paint in a scrubbing fashion to obtain color. Preparation of the paint prevents ruining the brush and causing frustration. Another suggestion in getting paint on the brush is to roll the bristles over the pigment, already softened, instead of pushing down until the metal ferrule is forced into the half-pan.

Watercolor is a medium that requires sensitivity in painting; a full brush of color, and a gentle touch, with less pressure, less scrubbing, and careful manipulation of the brush, will produce good watercolor paintings.

This chapter includes experiences in washes (solid and graded), wet-in-wet painting, wet-on-dry, dry-on-wet, dry-brush, spatter, textures, calligraphy and Oriental brush painting.

Advanced Grades and Adult Watercolor

High school and adult watercolorists will enjoy painting on professional watercolor paper, and classroom teachers may want to use it for their own work. Watercolor paper is purchased according to weight; for example, if a ream (500 sheets) of watercolor paper weighed 70 pounds on the scale, each sheet is called a 70-lb sheet. This particular weight is not too desirable since, when washes are applied, the thin sheet has a strong tendency to buckle, which is extremely discouraging. The 140-lb paper is the best weight since it is stronger and a good thickness for the artist. A much more expensive paper is the 300-lb stiff, board-like quality, chosen mostly by professional artists. Artists use watercolor paper either dry or wet. If a wet surface is preferred, simply hold the paper under the faucet until it is wet on both sides and sponge off surplus water. Place it on a drawing board or masonite and tape it down on all four sides; it will soon stretch taut. When the painting is finished and dry, remove the tape, revealing a ½" white border. This is helpful as a holding area and in having it matted.

For the ambitious student books on step-by-step watercolor procedure may be purchased in art stores at a reasonable price. The serious artist uses watercolor in tubes and, possibly to the surprise of the buyer, the colors vary in prices. Only a few colors are necessary for excellent results. In fact, a painting completed in two colors, burnt umber (brown) and ultramarine blue, can be a strikingly beautiful picture produced by the warm (brown) and cool (blue) pigments. Brushes are important; a medium-priced one is fine, but don't ruin your introduction with a brush that doesn't point and have a good spring. When the dry bristles are pressed with the thumb they should spring back into position, and when wet the bristles should remain together and not spread out.

Brief History

Watercolor has been used in Europe for many years, but it was during the 18th and 19th centuries that the British school of painting developed transparent watercolor to its peak. Some artists inked a sketch, applying transparent washes over the lines. The Oriental artists for centuries painted with sumi inks in black and colors of unusual brilliance. Their procedure was one of dedicated self-discipline in memorizing the subject matter in such detail that the model was not needed in the actual painting. The charm and delicacy of their brush work is distinctive and superb, including the fine art of calligraphy, often referred to as beautiful writing but also applied to single brush strokes— positive, brilliant, and perfect in manipulation. To enjoy this to its fullest watch an Oriental artist perform a demonstration, painting a bird, landscape or flowers. Opportunities are available in schools and art associations.

The objective of this chapter is to invite readers of any age to enjoy watercolor, respecting its potentials, the equipment, and the basic procedure, so that at least you will be handling the medium correctly. Learn to handle watercolor easily, relax with freedom, use a full brush of color, achieve a transparent quality utilizing the paper as an essential ingredient to the success of the painting. It is hoped that through exploring watercolor you will find it one of your favorite art activities and possibly your most successful medium.

lesson 1

Preparation of the Watercolor Worktable

Procedure:

Spread newspaper over the worktable to protect it; this allows freedom in painting and makes cleanup easier. For an efficient method in watercolor painting organize the equipment for a logical sequence of steps, in a confined space on the right side. This is a convenient arrangement for right-handed pupils; let the left-handed ones set up their own materials. Have everything within easy reach; the water container beside the opened box, with cover nearest you; the brush removed for use; cut pieces of white paper ready for color testing; handy tissue for excess water; and the drawing paper in front of you. The time spent in preparing for the lesson results in enjoyment and success (Fig. 5-1A). This arrangement makes painting easier for the child, as the brush is dipped first into the water, then the paints, the cover, the test paper and finally the actual painting.

The standard 9″ × 12″ white drawing paper is fine; hold it vertically, the tall way, so the brush strokes are shorter for the beginner. Some papers have a tendency to curl under and contract when painted off the edges. To prevent this, which is entirely optional, simply draw a ½″ border on all four sides. The dry edges keeps the paper flat when totally wet. In using real watercolor paper many artists first dip in it water, or hold it under the running faucet, letting the excess drip off (Fig. 5-1B). Tape it to the board; when finished, the painting will have a white border ready for handling and mounting.

Fig. 5-1A: Watercolor work table.

Fig. 5-1B: Wetting watercolor paper.

lesson 2

Washes, Solid and Graded

Procedure:

Solid Wash

This lesson can be an easy, pleasant experience, learning to make a solid middle tone all over the paper. White drawing paper is best. An essential ingredient for a solid wash is a large enough puddle of color, rather too much than not enough. Since the recessed section of the watercolor box is shallow and confined in proportion, use a small plastic cup or container. Begin by dipping the brush generously into the color. Do not wipe it against the jar, but immediately begin brushing the color on with a long firm, positive stroke. The lower edge will retain the water, leaving a ridge of rich color. Without rinsing the brush repeat this stroke, connecting the first one; continue this method until the paper is a solid middle tone. Once you start, do not stop, but proceed steadily with a full brush of color. It's easy because it's hard, in the sense that most beginners rebrush the strokes. This is not necessary if the brush is dripping with color. Try a solid wash, one with a white dry border and one without, whichever is easiest for you and has the best results (Fig. 5-2A).

Fig. 5-2A: Solid wash.

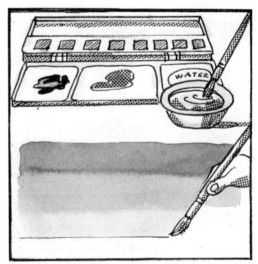

Fig. 5-2B: Graded wash.

Graded Wash (three values)

Select any color you wish and this time make two puddles in the cover of the box. One color will be the darkest, the second halfway between the darkest and white, a middle tone. The third value will be white paper, which is transparent watercolor's best friend. Start at the top with a very full brush of dark color and paint about a third of the way down; rinse the brush clean, and dip it into the middle wash another third down; finally rinse the brush again, dip it into clean water and wash part way down, leaving the rest dry white paper (Fig. 5-2B). Another method is to start with the dark color, diluting it as the wash is pulled down; this involves more rapid work, to keep the wash from drying in streaks. Both these lessons should be saved as backgrounds for themes in the wet-on-dry technique, such as free brush flowers, animals, landscapes, or even letters cut out for posters.

lesson 3

Wet-in-Wet Painting

Procedure:

This is one of those success lessons that both children and adults need to boost their morale in a new medium, besides developing freedom in wash and

Fig. 5-3A: Wet-in-wet technique background.   Fig. 5-3B: Wet-in-wet background, dried, with musical theme added.

color experimentation. Paint a bright wash over the paper. While it is soaking wet apply the brush, dripping with a different bright or dark color, onto the wet background, and watch it spread out in different shapes. Rinse the brush and add more colors. Hold the paper up at one side and let the colors run—but only for a brief time or the colors will mix and result in muddy tones. No two papers will be alike; notice the interesting patterns (Fig. 5-3A).

When the paper has dried, use it for a second lesson, planned around a motif suggested by the colors and pattern. This wet-in-wet suggested a musical theme—notes and a guitar—which was painted on with a small brush. Colored markers could be also used (Fig. 5-3B).

lesson 4

Fun with
Basic Geometric Forms

Procedure:

Invite the pupils to translate realistic forms—animals, heads, boxes, lamps, boats, etc.—into basic geometric shapes. Let them become acquainted with cubes, spheres, cylinders, egg and cone forms that are actually the basis of all objects. This will help them draw realistic forms and act as motivation for the lesson.

Continue to work with three values; the third again is the white paper. Sketch lightly in pencil five shapes—cube, cone, sphere, egg, and cylinder (Fig. 5-4A). Prepare two puddles of any color you prefer; be sure one is very dark, the other middle value. Direction of sunlight is important. In these examples, the light is on the left of the object so shadows will be cast to the right side. Shadows add drama and contrast to the painting, and at the same time encourage the students to create bright, sparkling pictures.

Two methods can be used to accent the sunlight side; one method is by outline and the second and preferred method is by a few brush strokes of middle tone in back of the sunlight side. Begin with either the middle or dark value; if the dark color is applied first then immediately paint in the shadow, since the brush is full of that color. Let the dark dry, then add the middle value; notice what a strong geometric shape is created.

When painting on the curved surface—cone, egg, sphere and cylinder—

be sure to run a clean, water wet brush on the edge of the middle value, which will round out the object in a more refined gradation.

Fig. 5-4A: Geometric forms in three values—
white-grey-black.

lesson 5

How to Paint a House from a Cube

Procedure:

Lightly sketch a cube and draw a roof on it. Indicate again the light source, from the left. Select a bright color, red for example; prepare a puddle of red and a puddle of the palest red (just a tint), plus a puddle of middle grey on the roof. Proceed as with the geometric cube, but this time add windows, door, foreground chimney and winding road. How simple a landscape, yet how effective. Now plan a group of houses, beginning with cubes in different positions, and paint your first composition (Fig. 5-5A).

Fig. 5-5A: Cube turned into house in three values.

lesson 6

Painting a Round Object

Procedure:

Painting a round object like an apple illustrates basic principles applicable to watercolor technique. An apple is actually a solid geometric sphere with a stem and leaf added, plus realistic coloring. Mix or prepare three puddles in the palette cover of red, yellow, and green, remembering that the highlights and background will remain white paper. Later, various background washes can be experimented with for color values and harmony. With a full brush of red color, practice left and right curves plus horizontal large and small curves for the top of the apple. Keeping this structure in mind paint the round apple at least three inches high, *no shorter*, for one of the biggest mistakes in water-color is to work too small, ruining all chances for freedom and full paint brush.

The apple could be sketched lightly in pencil first, for confidence in color application. While the paint is wet, fill in the circle, leaving sharp white highlights on the left side of the fruit and top shoulder of the apple, at the same time dragging out the shadow. With the brush still red with color dip the brush directly into the green puddle and repaint the shadow side and shadow; notice how it turns a brownish color. This is the result of mixing complements, red and green (Fig. 5-6A).

The secret of a polished looking apple is to have strong rich colors to begin with because watercolor dries lighter, quite different from tempera which remains the same due to its opaque quality. With this first fruit practice drawing your own still life and using your own color choice paint the entire group, adding appropriate shadows for contrast. Notice how simply the leaves are painted in single, not touching, strokes (Fig. 5-6B).

Fig. 5-6A: Sphere changed into apple.

Fig. 5-6B: Still life group.

lesson 7

Isolated Pictures

Procedure:

After experimenting with solid and graded washes it is good to explore the possibilities of leaving isolated areas without paint. This is essential in picture-making in the watercolor medium where white paper plays such an important part in adding sparkle. In a smaller area sketch a simple outline of a form you have decided upon. Then mix a puddle of color, and beginning at the top of the paper proceed to use the technique already explained and start the long strokes to make the wash, pulling it down gradually around the open area. Recall the importance of keeping each stroke full of color and joining the preceding stroke with the next one, creating a smooth even wash (Fig. 5-7A).

This first isolated picture is a monarch butterfly. When dry, add the beautiful design of lines, veins and dots.

Plan another picture in which the dry white isolated areas become clouds. When the wash has been completed soften the cloud with blue purple shadows, blurring the inner edge with a semi-wet brush (Fig. 5-7B). Decide on a motif to be used against the sky; an airplane seems ideal. This can be traced onto the watercolor cloud background and then painted in strong colors (Fig. 5-7C).

Fig. 5-7A: Water etching with accent design.

Fig. 5-7B: Wash background around isolated areas.

Fig. 5-7C: Isolated areas developed into clouds in completed airplane theme.

lesson 8

Textures in Watercolor

Procedure:

There are endless textures that can be created with watercolors. They are exciting, and challenge the imagination. Many are used by professional artists, as demonstrated in their finished work. Encourage the students to find various textures in famous art prints that are displayed in the room, and ask them to tell how they think each texture was created.

It is good practice to frequently take a full brush of color and paint uninterrupted strokes, rich in color and positive in pressure. Use a smaller brush, stroking long thin lines in all directions.

A popular texture in watercolor—but not to be overdone, and used only where it is appropriate—is the spatter technique. Fill the brush with color and tape it over a pencil or ruler. If the brush is too full, large unpleasant spots will result. Practice on scrap paper first (Fig. 5-8A). There are other ways of spattering. Use a piece of window screening and stroke the brush over it, or snap the bristles with the thumb or fingers.

Dry brush takes a little time on practice paper before the stroke is ready for the actual painting. Drag the brush across the practice paper, releasing paint until just enough pigment is left to create a series of fine hairlines.

A bolder and fascinating effect results from the use of a sponge. A household sponge, cut into small pieces and dampened first, is placed in the watercolor puddle. Then, holding it above the paper simply place it down firmly and lift it off to reveal a delicate, intricate, lacework pattern. For another effect, try turning the sponge after it is on the paper.

A different experience for the older and adult group, especially when using real watercolor paper, is to scrape the wet paint after a wash has been made. This is a good technique for sun sparkle on water in a seascape (Fig. 5-8B).

In adult and professional watercolor painting another material, namely Maskoid or Miskit, is frequently used. This is a blocking-out liquid that keeps white paper sparkling white and dry. To simulate this method in advanced school artwork, masking tape serves well and is less expensive. Directions are on the container of Maskoid; however, the correct way to use it is to wet and soap the brush, dip it into the liquid, and paint areas that are to be left white paper. Wash and rinse the brush, keeping it just for this particular liquid. It is then easy to wash over this part. When the painting is dry, erase or rub with a clean finger and the Maskoid will roll or peel off, leaving clean white paper. It is not wise—and looks definitely amateurish—to overuse this medium. Professionals use it for such details as clotheslines, small birds, fine distant birch trees and such additional details.

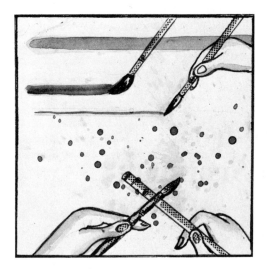

Fig. 5-8A: Varied strokes and spatter technique.

Fig. 5-8B: Dry brush sponge scrape.

Fig. 5-8C: Dry brush (sky); Maskoid (boat); masking tape (sail); wash (water).

Miskit is the same type of block-out liquid, but it is orange, allowing the artist quick recall where it is used. For advanced school art in watercolor painting, if Maskoid is too expensive, masking tape acts fairly well. Apply it firmly but not too hard; pull off at an angle slowly. It works well on watercolor paper but on drawing paper seems to pull the surface a little.

In Fig. 5-8C four distinct textures are used: Maskoid for the boat, masking tape for the mast and sail, dry brush for the windswept sky, and wash for the water with scraped highlights made by a single-edged razor blade.

lesson 9

Painting from Your Own Snapshot

Procedure:

Select one of your favorite snapshots (Fig. 5-9A) and sketch the composition on regular 140-lb watercolor, stretched on a board. Paint in the sky first, using the wet-in-wet method, then using a little Maskoid on the sparkling water. Complete the picture, remembering contrast. When the sky is dry add the branches and other dark accents (Fig. 5-9B). This is your own original watercolor. Good luck!

Fig. 5-9A: Actual snapshot—personal size.

Fig. 5-9B: Watercolor from snapshot.

lesson 10

Oriental Brushwork

Procedure:

Chinese or Oriental brushwork is well worth practicing and studying since so many of its principles are similar to transparent watercolor. The results are brilliant, fresh and easy, with dramatic full brush strokes. The regular watercolor brush is excellent to start with, and the most inexpensive paper, newsprint, can be used; 12″ × 18″ size is best for freedom in painting. As you become fascinated with this Oriental technique and advanced in its application, the bamboo #10 brush and Japanese rice paper (or any of the various papers used by Oriental artists), plus sumi ink, will yield beautiful pictures.

It is wise to study this technique in black and its gradations first, before becoming confused with color. The bamboo branch is a typical subject in this style of painting. Begin with a full brush of color and paint the sections first, leaving white space between the joints; again this adds sparkle to the painting when white paper is utilized as part of the design (Fig. 5-10A). In painting the leaves press the full brush down first, lifting it off to create a fine point. Do not repaint the leaf; keep it fresh and positive. Now draw the same subject matter again lightly, painting the bamboo stem in a middle value. The newsprint absorbs quickly so the dark leaves can be added immediately (Fig. 5-10B).

Fig. 5-10A: Basic bamboo stem.   Fig. 5-10B: Two-tone bamboo tree.

The Orientals have an organized procedure in their work, as observed in the painting of a bird (Fig. 5-10C). First, in the center of the paper they draw the eye, using a pointed brush held vertically, with the arm and wrist resting on the table for control. Then they draw the beak, followed by the back of the head, the body, tail feathers, wings, under part of body, legs and feet. Interestingly they draw the ground last. Even when a bird on a branch is being depicted, the bird is painted first in this methodic manner and the branch is painted last.

Flowers painted by the Chinese have a distinctive charm of their own; this can be observed in paperback books on Chinese painting that can be found in art stores. Advanced students and adults who attend a demonstration of this century-old art will gain valuable information and inspiration, and frequently will become so enthusiastic that they will go on to in-depth study. One of the most popular subjects of Chinese flower painting is the Chrysanthemum, whose petals, each of which grows from the center, provide an excellent lesson in brush control (Fig. 5-10D). The broad leaves are painted with full sweeping strokes, usually in three parts, later adding the veins with the point of the brush.

One lesson to learn from the Orientals is their habit of long meditation before painting. During this period they memorize the subject in detail, studying every position of the subject, so the painting itself is devoted entirely to technique and is not disturbed by constant examination of the model. Memory lessons would be a good practice for children and adults alike, leading to surprising results and enjoyable freedom of expression.

Fig. 5-10C: Bird, Oriental style.

Fig. 5-10D: Chrysanthemum brush strokes on Japanese rice paper.

chapter six

Creating Permanent Pictures in Brilliant Acrylic

Introduction

The terms *acrylic* and *polymer* are the scientific terms for plastic paints. Acrylic resin was first made in Germany in 1901 and later produced commercially in America in 1930. It is actually a modernized version of egg tempera, used by the early 13th-century Italian artists from Giotto through Botticelli—a medium consisting of egg yolk mixed with powdered paint. The 13th-century artists spent long hours of painstaking skill, patience and delicacy working with egg tempera. (Reference: *The Artist's Handbook of Materials and Techniques* by Ralph Meyer; Viking Press, New York, 1970.)

Acrylics and egg tempera have similar characteristics. They both become transparent as they dry, when used in a diluted state. Both have great durability, produce brilliant colors, and are beautifully executed with direct positive strokes. Neither egg tempera nor acrylics require a varnish, and they can be cleaned with mild soap and water. A special feature of acrylics is rapid drying, both for indoor and outdoor painting. There is no need to wait for parts of the painting to dry. A final attractive feature is that ready-prepared acrylic paint is available in tubes, jars and cartridge dispensers.

As in the case of other media, it is wise to plan before using this medium. The teacher should direct and guide pupils in prevention of wasted paint, paper, brushes and time. Without spending unnecessary money, everyone in class should be provided with a non-absorbent palette, such as an old plastic dinner plate, TV foil tray, stiff wax paper, varnished piece of wood or sheet of glass or metal with edges taped to protect the hands. Brushes can be nylon, oil bristles or watercolor, but keep them cleaned with water and mild soap, and while pupils are painting, have them keep brushes not in use in a water container to prevent them from hardening.

If a brush is left to dry with acrylic paint in it, the only way to remove the medium is to wash and rinse the brush with denatured alcohol. You can avoid this by keeping the brushes wet while in use, being sure they are washed with mild soap and water when finished, then drying them in an upright position. Any shallow wide-mouth can that does not tip over can be used as a water container.

One of the best ways to introduce acrylics is to have pupils begin on a small scale with practice strokes of diluted paint, overlapping to observe the transparent quality, trying thick strokes for texture and noticing the rapidity with which this medium dries as they continue work on a picture. It is best to have pupils become acquainted with acrylics by painting abstract deisgns. Do not burden them with immediate picture-making, but have them concentrate on the medium itself and all its potentials. A pupil cannot begin too young with this approach. Many times pupils try to accomplish too much before they have thoroughly investigated the procedure, leading only to confusion and sometimes a dislike for the medium. Enjoyment and understanding are the goals.

lesson 1

Newspaper Painting

Objectives:

Acrylics lend themselves well to endless techniques for all ages, in black and white and in color. Lessons in this chapter are developed to acquaint the pupil with the characteristics of this medium. They present ideas in various forms—cartoons, patterns, impasto, washes, monochromatic, toned paper, isolation pictures, textures and many others.

Materials (same throughout chapter six):

Acrylics can be purchased in tubes, jars and cartridge dispensers. Wooden craft sticks are excellent for lifting the paint out of jars, and should be used instead of brushes for this purpose. Water containers are essential, especially shallow tin cans that don't tip over or break. Acrylics can be painted on almost any surface as long as it is free from oil and grease, including papers, wood, textiles, wall surfaces, metal and stones. Adult and advanced school students can add sand or marble dust to the paint for texture. The palette need not be a specially purchased one; simply use an old plastic dinner plate, foil, wax paper, TV dinner tray, or any non-absorbent paper. Colors to begin with are the basic primary and secondary colors: yellow, red, blue, orange, green, purple plus black and white.

Procedure:

Newspaper is inexpensive, easily available, and ideal for early experiments in acrylics due to the fast-drying element of this medium. In preparation for this type of lesson ask the pupils to collect pages from the financial section where the print is free from bold black print and dark photographs. It is a good idea to have each young artist invert the page since the information printed is not needed; however, that is optional. Try to influence your pupils not to become too quickly involved with subject matter, rather, have them explore acrylics themselves first, discovering the potentials of this medium.

Begin by planning the size of your painting, allowing an inch margin for later trimming and mounting (Fig. 6-1A). An easy way and an economical procedure is to start with abstract, creative shapes. On the edge of a palette squeeze a small amount of acrylics; this is the reserve (Fig. 6-1B) from which paint is pulled into the center for mixing. Always dip the brush into the water to prepare it for the acrylic medium, then proceed with freebrush shapes, or lightly pre-penciled forms.

Create a pleasing arrangement of circles, squares, triangles, ovals, cylinders, or rectangles. Paint these in solid forms or in outline, adding textural effects such as dots, dashes, lines or curves with individual color placements

Fig. 6-1A: Use newspaper for drawing paper.   Fig. 6-1B: Squeeze acrylics on side of old plate, using the center for mixing.

(Fig. 6-1C). Try an all-over repeat pattern using bright colors, including alternate design and colors (Fig. 6-1D).

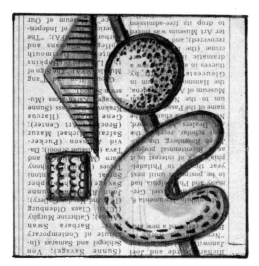

Fig. 6-1C: Abstract shapes on newspaper.   Fig. 6-1D: Allover repeat free brush pattern.

lesson 2

Monochromatic Pictures

Procedure:

Monochromatic means "of or having one color," and this method can also be economical in terms of paint and paper. Because of the absorption quality of newspaper, a fluid acrylic paint will run into the paper, causing a grading of tones. This is well demonstrated in the composition of three pine trees on a snowy landscape (Fig. 6-2A). Plan the trees in three sizes—the largest near the front edge of the paper, the middle size part way up, and the smallest tree on a distant hill. This proportion element is the beginning of perspective.

Another form of perspective is produced by the use of color. Since pine trees are green, you may experiment with various shades of green to produce perspective, or use green with black and white. The nearest tree is the darkest and brightest, so add a little black to the green; the middle tree can have a speck of white added, making it lighter; adding still more white to the small tree makes it seem to recede farther into the distance.

When using color, the rule is that warm colors (reds, yellows and oranges) advance, while cool colors (blues, greens and violets) recede. This lesson can be used successfully in the grades in teaching "near and far" theory.

Another dramatic monochromatic theme is a nighttime seascape showing moonlight on a sailboat and waves. Again, select a color to fit the mood—violet or blue. Prepare three values of the color on the palette and pre-plan the drawing lightly in pencil. Add white and black accents. (Fig. 6-2B).

Fig. 6-2A: Monochromatic landscape—
pine trees.

Fig. 6-2B: Monochromatic seascape.

lesson 3

Clowns and Fish on Newspaper

Procedure:

Motivation is essential in the grades, but in fact almost any age group can use a stimulus in artwork. Exhibit clown or fish pictures in the classroom while you discuss color, shapes and textures. You can remove the pictures for a memory lesson or let your pupils look at them further while they prepare their own pictures. In this activity a pre-planned pencil drawing would be helpful. Encourage the use of brilliant colors, again using black and white accents. A wide range of colors is not necessary; the basic primary colors—red, yellow and blue—are good for a clown face. Fig. 6-3A illustrates such a clown. Your pupils will also enjoy painting the fish (Fig. 6-3B).

Fig. 6-3A: Colorful clown portrait.

Fig. 6-3B: Imaginary fish.

lesson 4

Dark Wash over White or Pastel Acrylics

Procedure:

Since white paper is used, lightly pencil in the composition—a group of flowers. Then apply white acrylic paint in fairly thick consistency on the flowers. Mix a middle tone wash and brush over the entire paper, including the blossoms; this will produce a soft greyed effect. Accent the arrangement with dark stems and leaves by painting with a small brush (Fig. 6-4A).

Fig. 6-4A: Dark wash over white or pastel acrylic.

lesson 5

Impasto Flower Arrangement

Procedure:

Impasto means a heavy application of paint, made with a brush, stick or painting knife. Combining thinly painted areas with impasto lends character and texture to a painting. Begin to experiment with color harmonies to stimulate and challenge imagination. An interesting color theory is the *analogous* theory, involving the use of adjacent hues on the color chart. For example, starting with green, make use of its neighbors—blue, violet and red. For a more refined color scheme use the intermediate colors—green, green-blue, blue, blue-violet, and violet. Each art work will be different in this lesson since it involves free application and imagination. Prepare the colors on the palette in separate patches around the edge of the plate, then mix a wash of your color choice, brushing over the surface with a larger brush. Crush a tissue into a tight ball, dip it into the thick paint on the edge of the palette and press down onto the wash in groups, making thick applications of the paint. Arrange the colors to please you in large and small blossoms, finishing by adding fine stems and leaves (Fig. 6-5A).

Trees make another excellent subject for impasto work. The autumn season would make a strikingly brilliant picture, especially where the colors are pressed in pure application and not mixed together, except for shadow areas. Neither black nor white is used; to obtain a dark color simply mix complements red and green (Fig. 6-5B).

Fig. 6-5A: Impasto flowers.

Fig. 6-5B: Impasto autumn trees.

lesson 6

Animals on Grey and Black Paper

Procedure:

Grey and black construction paper offer a change from the constant use of white drawing paper. Try some animal shapes on black or grey. Children like to draw animals, are not concerned with accurate realism, and enjoy experimenting with different background color. Encourage pupils to draw a variety of positions rather than the usual side view or profile.

Introduce the idea of including one full view of an animal and partial views of others. The squirrel is a good animal to use for this since it is made up of ovals: head, body, eyes, ears and curved tail. For the squirrels, use grey paper with black, white and brown colors. To develop a rounded three-dimensional effect, paint a stroke of thick white paint on the back and immediately dip the brush into water and blend the paint over the back. Much of the white will be absorbed into the grey background. Add brown paint, using the same method, and finally complete the picture with fur texture made with fine lines painted with a smaller brush (Fig. 6-6A).

On black paper, plan an illustration in white paint showing birds at night in a snowstorm (Fig. 6-6B), or one in brilliant colors showing tropical birds, using paint thick and then thin for contrast.

Fig. 6-6A: Squirrel on grey paper.

Fig. 6-6B: White birds on black paper.

lesson 7

Oriental Brush Design

Procedure:

To introduce Oriental brushwork, white paper is best. Fill a large brush with dark, bright color mixed to a creamy fluid, and simply press the brush down on the paper from tip to heel (the heel is the part nearest the metal ferrule). This imprint is impressive if left alone; do not rework it, as the tip of the brush deposits a dark rich pigment while the remainder of the printed brush becomes diluted and sometimes leaves just an outline of the heel of the brush.

Continue making Oriental brush imprints, using different colors, but keep each stroke separate. Add accented stems and dots with a fine brush (Fig. 6-7A).

Fig. 6-7A: Oriental brush design.

lesson 8

Isolation Pictures

Procedure:

Another success lesson for individual expression is centered on "isolation pictures," in which tape is used to isolate areas from washes. Adhere gently with enough pressure so a wash will not run underneath but not so tight that it will tear the paper upon removal. Place these varied length strips of tape in different positions—vertical, horizontal, and diagonal—overlapping a few of them. Mix a diluted bright color and wash over the tapes. While still wet dip the brush into full strength acrylic and touch the wet wash; it will immediately spread out. Using the wooden end of the paint brush draw out paint from this small puddle, creating long curving lines radiating from the spot. Make other dots of different colors and repeat the method. Let the paint dry, then pull off the tape slowly, revealing isolation areas of sharp white paper. Add a few more wet spots, pulling out lines as before but overlapping some of the white unpainted strips. The effect is abstract and unusual and results in a classroom full of exciting pictures (Fig. 6-8A).

A different type of isolation picture is one using rubber cement. A lesson in this technique would be better for an older group on three counts: (1) rubber cement evaporates rapidly; (2) the odor may not be pleasing to younger groups; (3) there is more expense involved. Plan a small area to work on and freely brush strokes with rubber cement in different directions, then immediately

Fig. 6-8A: Isolation abstraction.

Fig. 6-8B: Rubber cement free brush abstraction.

Fig. 6-8C: Conventional fish design from
        abstraction.

screw cap on container. When this is dry, paint a bright-colored wash over the entire picture. Notice how the paint resists the cement, leaving deposits of color on the brush strokes (Fig. 6-8B).

To challenge their imaginations, ask pupils to turn the paper around into different positions and try to discover subject matter—boats, birds, animals, people, fish, or fruits. If the teacher makes a list of ideas on the board, this can help the student to visualize elements. In Fig. 6-8C fish appeared to be swimming around, so a piece of tracing paper was placed over the previous painting and the fish drawn in bold lines; this was in turn transferred to another drawing paper. With strong textural lines in various colors the composition was completed as a conventional interpretation of the abstract isolated painting.

lesson 9

Dual Picture Cutout

Procedure:

Use white paper for the background and colored construction paper for the cutout. In Fig. 6-9A the house and road join and are cut out as one unit. The theme could be correlated with the curriculum or a seasonal theme: pumpkins and autumn leaves, bells and holly, etc. Place a pad of newspapers on the work table and pin the cutout with common pins to keep it close to the drawing

Fig. 6-9A: House and road cutout washed over.

paper. Paint a realistic background in colors of your choice directly over the entire picture, cutout included. Let it dry, then remove the house and road pattern. Plan strong sunlight from one direction, in this case from the left; add white paint to any areas where the wash crept through. Leave the left side of the house white, painting the shadow side blue; complete the picture with accents of grass, bark, trees, hills and shadows. Save the cutout for the next lesson.

lesson 10
Collage and Counterchange

Procedure:

This lesson, a continuation of lesson nine, uses the cutout house and road to create a combination of collage and counterchange. On the newspaper pad paint the cutout a rich black with acrylic paint; again the beauty of this paint is its rapid drying quality. The definition of *collage* in art terms is "an extension of the technique of papiers collés developed by the surrealist painter Max Ernst." A collage means a picture composed of papers or other elements pasted on; in fact a single bit of paper pasted on a composition becomes a collage. Counterchange is usually concerned with black and white, therefore a counterchange picture is one where black exchanges place with white. These are dramatic effects used often in advertising art; posters and lettering are ideal subjects for counterchange.

Fig. 6-10A: Collage and counterchange with cutout.

Fig. 6-10B: Collage and counterchange.

In Fig. 6-10A the house and road can be used as a farm theme by planning a near farmhouse with a weathervane on top. Notice that the black turns to white when it enters the black area and white becomes black on the white parts of the picture. In Fig. 6-10B a swirled background is drawn in pencil first, then a lighthouse is planned in pencil over the background. Begin using black paint and counterchange the lighthouse by changing it to black as it enters the white area; reverse it so it changes to white in the black swirl.

lesson 11

Acrylic Printing with Kitchen Items

Procedure:

Here is an opportunity to use a different color harmony—this time one of brilliant contrasts based on the complementary theory: red and green, blue and orange, and yellow and violet. On the color chart these double colors are opposite each other, or in other words they complement each other, and when used in posters or printing projects the result is one of sharp, strong, contrasts. Select a pair of colors and squeeze them out on the palette; then selecting a

Fig. 6-11A: Acrylic printing, using kitchen items.

plastic fork, dip the tines into the red and print wherever you wish. Clean the tines and press them into the opposite color, green, and without wiping off the green press another print. You will notice an almost black color where the two colors, red and green, mixed. So you find that with two opposite colors, three will be produced. Try other objects: end of a small spool, end of a pencil, end of plastic spoon handle, small paper cup (both rim and base), and finally a pipe cleaner twisted into the shape of a bird's foot (Fig. 6-11A).

lesson 12

Sgraffito on Black and White Paper

Procedure:

Sgraffito, as mentioned earlier, means to scratch through. Mix a grey color to a creamy consistency, not a thin wash, and freely brush white paper. In places the paint will drag, showing broken white areas; leave these for interesting textural effects. Let your painting dry. Cut a short piece of cardboard about $3'' \times 3''$ and notch the edge (Fig. 6-12A). Dip the notched edge into thick white acrylic paint and draw it over the grey background with sweeping lines (Fig. 6-12B). Try black paper with white and colored paint, stroking in different and opposite directions (Fig. 6-12C). Use these techniques in a realistic theme such

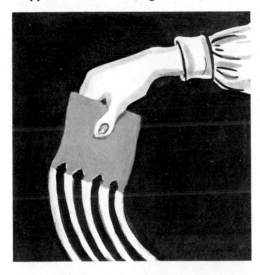

Fig. 6-12A: Producing sgraffito technique.

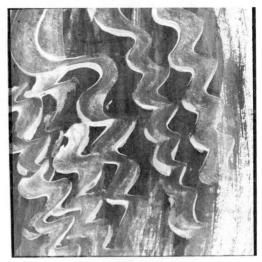

Fig. 6-12B: White over grey.

as a seascape, with windswept black sky and a turbulent ocean, adding small sailboats leaning in the wind on the horizon (Fig. 6-12D).

In using the sgraffito techniques, pre-plan the theme with a good deal of thought. In fact that could be a lesson in itself—making many sketches in pencil and cutting the cardboard with notches for the scratching effect, in preparation for the lesson in acrylics.

Fig. 6-12C: White over black.

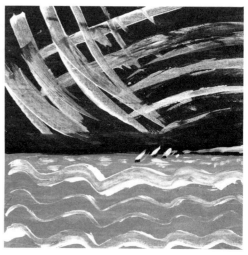

Fig. 6-12D: Dramatic sgraffito seascape.

chapter seven

Dramatic Conté Crayon Effects

Brief History and Characteristics of Conté Crayon

Conté crayon derives its name from a Frenchman, Nicolas Jacques Conté (1755–1805), originally trained as a painter, who had a tremendous talent for inventing. Need for his talent arose when the French supply of natural graphite for drawing pencils was cut off by a war with England. Conté produced a mixture of clay and graphite for pencils which is still used today.

The early Conté crayon was available in black, white, sepia and sanguine, but today a wide range of colors can be purchased not only in stick form but in wood-cased pencils as well. It comes in varying degrees of hardness; (HB) hard; (B) medium; and (2B) soft. The pure Conté stroke is best obtained with the hard and medium grade. There are twelve 2½" sticks to a box. These when broken in half are a good size for the child to hold, and a box will supply an average class of 24 pupils.

Introduction

Just as fingerpaint can be successfully enjoyed at junior and senior high school level, Conté crayon can be explored in the lower grades. Children can be taught quickly the beauty of Conté crayon, learning the soft colors, the sharp lines and the sensitive shadings this medium can produce. To understand this crayon the pupil should think of it as fun and explore it with freedom. Through

115

individual experimentation he will develop a familiarity with the wide variety of strokes and colors that will lead to self-confidence. Any child can easily be discouraged with a new tool if he does not know what to expect, and such discouragement can block progress. Guidelines should be provided through discussion and illustrated demonstrations as, for example, a discussion on the necessity for positive and direct strokes that are not worked over. You should also point out to the pupil how details of sharp dark accents can enrich the drawing. Details such as veins on a leaf can be added; features can be brightened; or the pupil can show petals turning, shadows, and three-dimensional effects.

Pupils in the upper grades will enjoy the unexpected results obtained by twisting and turning the crayon, rather than letting one stroke do all the work; adding pressure to either side of the tool; cutting notches for increased lines; and other different procedures.

Experimenting with abstract forms can challenge the child's imagination in creating birds, houses, animals, people, and even a new look in lettering. Toned papers increase dramatic effects; for example, white Conté crayon on brown or colored paper with black sharp accents make strikingly brilliant displays.

Helpful Suggestions with Conté Crayon
That Produce Greater Success

1. Use the least expensive paper—newsprint. The 12″ × 18″ size is best.
2. Always have a pad of at least 20 sheets of newspaper under the drawing. Be sure it is free from wrinkles, tears, and any particles that may be left inside. A double precaution is to iron these sheets and tape them together. Stack these away just for Conté crayon work.
3. Most materials have some problem. Conté crayon smudges easily, and the color is easily transfered to the fingers. Use the easy dish detergent method of pouring some liquid into the palms of the hands and rubbing it thoroughly into the hands, especially under the nails and around the cuticles. It leaves a pleasant feeling. Let it dry before working with the crayon. When the drawing lesson is over wash the hands, creating warm suds that quickly clean off the crayon.
4. Spraying the drawing is not necessary while practicing, but on a final picture spray at intervals to prevent smudging. Spray with the windows open or step out into the corridor.
5. If your pupils concentrate on the center of the paper, they can allow for expansion of their themes and later trim off unwanted paper before the drawing is mounted.
6. Buy a can of fixative for charcoal and pencil, and follow directions on

the can. Hold it at least 12″ away from picture, moving the container constantly. Don't flood the work. Hold picture upright.

7. A reminder: if your pupils stand when drawing they can apply more pressure to the strokes, creating that black sharp edge with beautiful shadings.

8. Start the younger grades with a short, half piece of crayon; let the junior and senior high school level use the whole piece. Never discard broken pieces as they can always be used for small accents.

lesson 1

Basic Vertical, Horizontal and Curved Strokes

Objectives:

The materials are few; the results are multiple. Conté crayon is dependent upon the pressure of the individual strokes. Learning these basic strokes and hand positions will open a new world with this crayon of many shadings.

Materials:

(Since the materials are the same throughout the chapter, they need not be repeated for each lesson.)

Conté crayons in three degrees of hardness: HB (hard); B (medium); 2B (soft). These come packed 12 to a box, in four colors: black, white, red, and sanguine.
Conté crayons in pastel colors, called Conté pastels, in a box of 24 hues.
A pad of newspaper (at least 20 sheets).
Fixative.
12″ × 18″ newsprint.
Paper towels for wiping hands.

Procedure:

Holding the paper with one hand at the top so it won't slip, grasp the crayon in the center of the long stick and pull toward you, creating a wide shaded band (Fig. 7-1A). Repeat, practicing until a shaded page results. Don't discard this sheet; it will be good to use in adding different strokes. Many pupils will find standing a better working position than sitting since more pressure can be applied.

Again hold a new sheet of paper at the top, pulling the crayon down, but this time use the narrow side, resulting in a ¼"-wide stroke. Try making steady straight lines (Fig. 7-1B). Try breaking these lines into dash or brick patterns, horizontally and vertically.

Holding the Conté crayon for the next stroke is a little more difficult, but the results are distinctive. Grasp the crayon on the two sides on the edges, drawing with a down stroke on one sharp edge (Fig. 7-1C). This is the beginning of many exciting developments to follow.

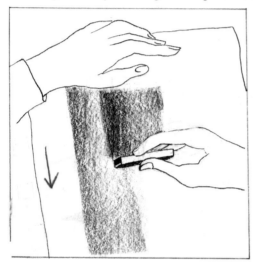

Fig. 7-1A: Shading technique.

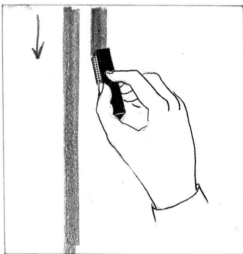

Fig. 7-1B: Narrow side drawing.

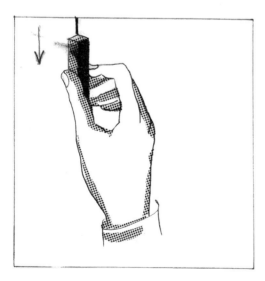

Fig. 7-1C: Drawing with edge.

Using this third position again draw on the edge, pulling the crayon downward, but swing out to the left in a wide fan shape. Notice how the shading changes—and if enough pressure has been applied, a bright, sharp, black edge will result. Try moving to right and left as you proceed down the sheet (Fig. 7-1D). Now try holding the paper at the base and push up.

For the sharp distinctive Conté crayon stroke that no other crayon will yield, try applying pressure to the *up* and *back* stroke, pulling down after each UP movement (Fig. 7-1E). Next try the same motion but to right, left and right, moving downward. Make short, in-place, zig-zag strokes, and by keeping the hand in the same position but moving the paper you will make circular designs.

Now that the crayon is becoming more familiar, hold it sideways on the edge and move it to the right for a fine line, then curve down, across to the left, and down again until a wavy, watery texture is seen (Fig. 7-1F).

You will now experience more freedom with wider arch-like strokes. Begin by starting at the left side of the paper, and with a free-arm movement

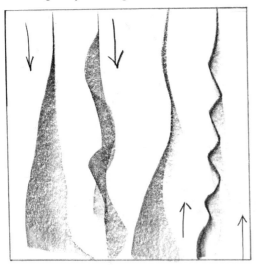

Fig. 7-1D: Swinging strokes.

Fig. 7-1E: Zig-zag effects.

make expanding circular strokes. Notice the sharp black edges contrasted to the varying degrees of shading (Fig. 7-1G).

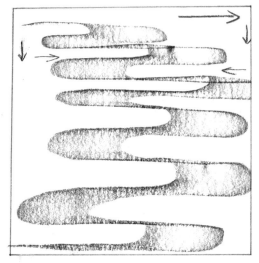

Fig. 7-1F: Watery effects.

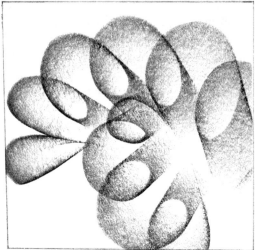

Fig. 7-1G: Arching strokes.

lesson 2

Exploring Everyday Objects

Objectives:

In drawing objects be sure the class is familiar with them—and also likes them; this makes a big difference in attitudes. Clear sharp photographs on the bulletin boards provide excellent resource material. Such stimulation can increase the child's enthusiasm throughout the lesson. A new treatment, the notched edge, is introduced in this chapter.

Procedure:

Boats and water are ideal subjects for this medium. The mast and sail are made in one stroke. Begin with the corner of the crayon, bear down as it is pulled to the right and sweep the crayon to the left for the full sail. A flip of the end of the crayon produces the flag, and a horizontal stroke shapes the hull of the boat. The water is simply a series of wavy strokes, pressed down on the

edge for hard dark accents. Keep the boats and the waves darker in the foreground and lighter grey in the distance. Fig. 7-2A illustrates this principle. Add
people.

The profile of the butterfly makes an interesting picture. Study of the
hundreds of kinds of butterflies may already have been undertaken, and this
would be a good opportunity to record them in Conté crayon. Further brilliant
color accents could be made with poster paints when the Conté has been
sprayed (Fig. 7-2B).

Fig. 7-2A: Study of sails.

Fig. 7-2B: Butterfly sketch.

Fig. 7-2C: Fish in line and shade.

Fishes of all sizes and shapes (Fig. 7-2C) give endless joy to children, and are found everywhere—books, field trips, movies, and some children have aquariums in their homes. Here is a new use of the Conté crayon—it is notched to make multiple lines. The teacher could cut a few notches first to illustrate how gently it should be done, for too much pressure will cut the crayon in half. Try other ideas with the notched edge: cutouts close together, far apart, equal, deep and shallow (Fig. 7-2D). The effects are beautiful and its uses numerous.

Use the notched crayon on the fish; it will look like the one in Fig. 7-2E. Every school child likes to draw pictures of clowns, and a portrait of a clown can make a colorful room decoration. To encourage the class the teacher can display many bright clear photographs of clowns—full-length figures, profiles and front face. The clown in Fig. 7-2F started with a sphere, with features, hat and ruffle easily added with short pieces of Conté crayon.

Trees and landscapes make an ideal subject matter since the beauty of this crayon yields bright and soft shadings. In discussing trees impress upon the children the necessity of drawing as the tree grows, from the earth upward. This time hold the paper at the bottom edge and push the crayon upward, lifting off as the branch thins and becomes lighter in color (Fig. 7-2G).

A good procedure in drawing landscapes, especially in Conté crayon, is to pre-plan the scene, in light pencil. Then draw in the distant rolling hills in lighter grey for atmosphere; next darken the bushes and grasses nearest you. Finally draw in the tree. Use the short crayon with notches for bark or invent your own way to show the roughness.

Greeting cards can look exceptionally attractive with the Conté shading. Combine your lettering lesson with a birthday message as in Fig. 7-2H. Spray

Fig. 7-2D: Notched crayon effect.

Fig. 7-2E: Fish made with notched crayon.

it, mount on gay colored paper, and the recipient will marvel at its professional and distinctive appearance.

The seasonal card makes a delightful greeting with candle motifs, enhanced with sparkling rays and crisp holly leaves (Fig. 7-2I).

Fig. 7-2F: Notched crayon clown.

Fig. 7-2G: Tree study.

Fig. 7-2H: Greeting card design.

Another easy twisted crayon motion creates beautiful modern candle glow in this card, which shows three candles with extended rays (Fig. 7-2J).

Fig. 7-2I: Christmas card design.

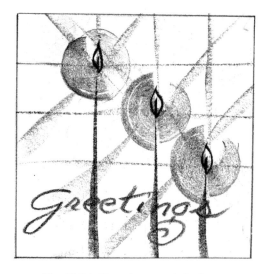

Fig. 7-2J: Greeting card design.

lesson 3

Fruits, Vegetable and Flowers

Objectives:

The previous lessons have built up basic skills and understanding of this crayon, and I hope pleasure as well, since it is through actual application that any medium can be discovered. In Chapter 5, lesson 4, geometric shapes were explored, and now these can be applied to this lesson.

Procedure:

Draw a sphere lightly at first to establish the position; add a shadow. Now redraw, this time over the apple, making it look like a real natural fruit rather than a round ball. One of the most beautiful apples to draw is the Delicious; study the ones you like. Assume the light is from the left and darken the fruit, leaving a highlight on the left side (Fig. 7-3A). Add a stem, a leaf, and a shadow.

Since you have drawn the apple so well, try a pear, which is merely a small apple on top of a larger one (Fig. 7-3B). Don't forget the shadow on the right to give strength to the picture.

Grapes are miniature oval apples, but think of the bunch of grapes as a whole unit. Sketch in pencil, lightly, the general contour of the total grapes,

Fig. 7-3A: Apple.

Fig. 7-3B: Pear.

and then, pressing down on the edge of a short crayon, plan the grapes (Fig. 7-3C).

The pumpkin lends itself well to Conté crayon and is easy to make by turning the paper in different positions. For your strokes, the curved ridges fall in place if the back ones are drawn in first. A thick stem and bold dark shadow emphasize the weight of the vegetable. For seasonal classroom displays, brown or sepia Conté on orange paper with black worked into the grooves and shadows is striking (Fig. 7-3D).

The cylinder comes into use again in the daffodil. The flower should be lightly placed in pencil first so the petals will appear to grow from the center and not at unrelated angles. Plan the trumpet, first the cylinder and then the ruffle; add the petals, bearing down on the edges for sharpness and accent; then add the stem and delightful long leaves, drawing from the base of the paper upward (Fig. 7-3E).

Fig. 7-3C: Bunch of grapes.

Fig. 7-3D: Pumpkin.

The pussywillow is another natural, especially when drawn on blue paper with white, black and sepia crayons. Again it is wise to plan the branches so the composition will be established and all concentration given to the technique (Fig. 7-3F).

All children have imagination and it should be encouraged. The flower is a good subject because all the stroke techniques you have learned can create unusual, beautiful and distinctive blossoms. Let your classroom boast the most spectacular blooms. Use the notched crayon for this flower (Fig. 7-3G).

Fig. 7-3E: Daffodil.

Fig. 7-3F: Pussywillow.

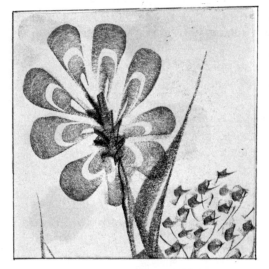

Fig. 7-3G: Flower, using notched crayon.

lesson 4

People, Birds,
Animals and Portraits

Objectives:

The aim of this chapter is to use our everyday resources as subject matter and try to interpret these subjects with Conté crayon. Children enjoy drawing people and the classroom is an ideal place to use a variety of models. This is the motivation they need—discussing the action, the clothes, the proportions of figure without any set goal but rather insuring freedom of expression. Birds and animals are excellent material for this medium as well as for portraits.

Procedure:

Here is a good time to use broken Conté crayons for the head, feet, hands. Action figures can tell a story. Let the class decide on their own. The subject used is a boy walking fast on a cold day with hat and scarf. For the older level discuss the basic body proportions, length of arms, size of head, etc. Begin with the head, but do not be concerned with the face; draw in the jacket with two broad strokes; then the legs, one stroke each; then the shoes, hat and scarf. Add a shadow under and in back of the figure to add strength to the picture (Fig. 7-4A). Next try other action poses of boys and girls.

You may want to draw a portrait; if so, you must study the features, facial proportions and hair treatment. In Fig. 7-4B the face is drawn first on the left side, then on the right, leaving the center in highlight. Use only two strokes for the sides of the face; the center white paper adds the contrast it needs. The hair is made with five long sweeping strokes as illustrated, with four short strokes for the bangs on the forehead. Six strokes complete the collar and shoulders; now the features are added very simply.

Due to the texture of feathers, birds can be drawn well in this medium. In Fig. 7-4C the bill is drawn first, then the head, back, tail feathers, breast and legs. The grass is added, and last the round eye is accented with a pointed crayon.

All children enjoy watching the squirrel with his fluffy tail, rounded body, small ears and dark eyes. Plan to sketch this little animal so it is well spaced on the paper. Proper center placement will allow room for the bushy tail. Begin with the head, then draw the body, paws, and tail, and last the tree branch, adding texture to the bark by running the edge of the crayon up and down (Fig. 7-4D).

The cat is similar to the squirrel in roundness with ears a little more pointed, and a long narrow tail so easy to sweep in. Draw the cat looking in the opposite direction, rather than repeating the same position each time (Fig. 7-4E).

Fig. 7-4A: Action figure of boy.

Fig. 7-4B: Portrait of girl.

Fig. 7-4C: Bird.

The elephant, another favorite of children, may be sketched easily. Draw the face and trunk first, then the large ears, rounded back, wide heavy legs, large toenails and tusks (Fig. 7-4F).

The duck is drawn very much the same way as the bird. Begin with the duck's bill, then draw in the head, back, tail feathers, water and grasses (Fig. 7-4G).

Fig. 7-4D: Squirrel.

Fig. 7-4E: Cat.

Fig. 7-4F: Elephant.

Wild animals make excellent subjects. Let's start with the leopard, but try the others as well. Again a sphere is drawn for the head, sweeping the crayon on either side of the head. Add short round ears, and a broad flat nose (left white or white can be used here). Add the slanted eyes and strong chin, using the stroke techniques we have explored (Fig. 7-4H).

The horse is another animal that makes a good Conté crayon subject. Concentrate on the long nose first, the flat cheeks, wide open nostrils and forelock. Add the pointed ears and mane in bold positive strokes (Fig. 7-4I).

Fig. 7-4G: Duck.

Fig. 7-4H: Leopard.

Fig. 7-4I: Horse.

Look at pictures of horses running, standing, jumping—and with a small crayon lightly sketch in an outline of the pose, just as a light guide. Then plunge in with strong strokes, forgetting about the faint underdrawing (Fig. 7-4J). Conté crayon is not used to fill in spaces as in coloring books but rather to create the shadings and black sharp edges. Try a Palomino drawn with white crayon on brown paper and blended accents of sepia or dark brown or even black for contrast (Fig. 7-4K). Experiment with all sorts of animals, but work large enough to control the Conté crayon.

The lower grades could try animals on large paper. Encourage them to use broad, sweeping lines, pressing down on the crayon to produce a variety of tones.

Fig. 7-4J: Palomino.

Fig. 7-4K: Palomino head.

chapter eight

Working with Felt Tip Pens

Introduction

Felt tip pens, commonly called markers, are so familiar to your pupils in everyday use that they serve as an excellent medium in art classes. This medium is quick drying; yields brilliant, bold colors; gives instant response with light pressure; comes in a variety of points; and offers the desirable double quality of permanence and water-solubility. Felt tip pens are excellent in lessons where direct, positive strokes are needed and are especially adaptable for accents and detail work.

Suggestions for correct use and longer life of felt tip pens:

1. Do not use markers to fill in extra large areas; it only uses up ink, where another medium would serve as well.
2. When not in use, replace cap.
3. Keep away from clothing.
4. Use on dry paper, not wet. After the water-soluble pen is drawn on the dry paper, wet the edges to release color.
5. To prevent ink from staining through to other paper underneath, place a sheet of wax or tracing paper under drawing.
6. Cover work area with newspaper as an added precaution.

These suggestions should not discourage the pupil but rather should make him aware of the characteristics of this medium. Markers are ideal for posters, lettering, cartoons, greeting cards, textural effects, and designs, and they combine well with other media. There are a variety of pens on the market, from fine tips to 2″ width, plus white markers. A circle compass that holds felt tip pens is also available.

lesson 1

Exploring Permanent and Water-soluble Pens

Procedure:

This book has stressed the importance of not plunging into picture-making until the medium is understood; if this suggestion is followed enjoyable and successful artwork will result for all ages. A welcome feature in working with felt tip pens is the use of smaller sheets of paper, both for economy and use of the marker. To explore both permanent and water-soluble pens, begin by drawing geometric shapes in a pleasing composition, in pencil lightly, planning where the solid black areas will be placed to balance the arrangement. Outline the shapes in pleasing colors. Dip a brush into clean water, and on the water-soluble shapes paint from the edges into the spaces. The color will immediately run. Keep within the lines; try another where the wash extends beyond; explore all possibilities. When dry add stipple technique to the design by holding the pen vertically and dotting in an area with a close polka dot effect (Fig. 8-1A).

Fig. 8-1A: Exploring with permanent and
water-soluble markers.

lesson 2

Formal Balance Design

Procedure:

Fold a small piece of paper in half (4″ × 6″ math paper is a good size); on the folded edge draw swirls, circles, ovals, and curved shapes extending outward; turn the folded paper over to the plain side, hold it up to the window and trace the other half as it shows through. Open the paper to find a complete formal balance, with each side alike. This design can be planned with precision, or it can be a free-flowing pattern. Graphite the back of this design by rubbing a soft pencil over it, then place it on white drawing paper and trace the design. When it is lifted off a complete design is ready to redraw with a water-soluble marker, any color of your choice. Paint each shape separately with small brush dipped in clean water (Fig. 8-2A). When dry, another color can be used for accents and texture if desired.

Fig. 8-2A: Formal balance design.

lesson 3

Greeting Cards

Procedure:

Making greeting cards is usually a popular activity in the classroom and this type of lesson would only involve colored markers and white paper. Experiment with folding the paper in different ways for more exciting cards. Plan the design lightly in pencil on scrap paper, and when a good idea is developed transfer the sketch to white paper. If you want the color to run into a soft wash do not use colored construction paper, as it seems to stop the process of spreading; besides, white is a good contrast to multicolors and black. Birthday cards are ideal for a classroom; simple floral motifs can be imaginary and creative (Fig. 8-3A). Attractive cards can be made with permanent markers in color, using clearcut designs and scalloped edges.

Fig. 8-3A: Attractive birthday card, featuring clearcut design with scalloped edge.

lesson 4

Cartoons

Procedure:

All ages enjoy making cartoons and reference material is available everywhere, in daily newspaper and magazines. However, encourage the pupils to invent their own characters. Again, sketch the idea first. Sports offer endless ideas, such as the amateur golfer (Fig. 8-4A). The water-soluble pen is best for this illustration since wetting the outline creates a shading, effective in this form of art.

Fig. 8-4A: The bewildered golf amateur
makes a good cartoon subject.

lesson 5

Impressionism (Inspired by French Modern Art)

Procedure:

Illustrating the work of French Modern Artists with felt tip pens can be stimulating, especially where the artists believed in brilliant colors and direct strokes. Four areas will be briefly touched on in this chapter: impressionism, pointillism, cubism and expressionism. Such famous painters as Monet, Renoir, Cézanne and later Seurat were leaders in this movement of modern art in Europe. There were numerous phases and styles that developed from their work, but these four provide a good introduction to the class and a chance for pupils to experiment in the actual techniques involved.

The impressionistic theory was based on two principles: (1) The artist should try to capture the fleeting atmospheric "impressions" of nature, seen for the first time, in relation to constantly changing light. Impressionists insisted on painting "on the spot" and frowned on studio work from memory, notes or sketches. This is also called "plein-air" art, which means art painted outdoors. (2) The second principle was that the artist should use only the spectral colors (red, orange, yellow, green, blue and violet), with no brown or black. Fig. 8-5A is a perfect example of impressionism—a picture painted by looking out of the window on a winter's day and painting the tree, shadows and fence in bold, direct applications of spectral colors.

Fig. 8-5A: Impressionism painting on the spot
as opposed to working in the studio
from sketches or photographs.

lesson 6

Pointillism (Dot Pictures)

Procedure:

The artist recognized for developing this technique is Georges Seurat. He did not paint in lines or masses, but rather in dabs and dots. To create an after-image of orange, he would place dots of red next to dots of yellow, without letting the two colors touch. To see how this optical illusion works, cut out a 5″ circle; paint half red and the other half yellow (or use colored construction paper instead). Pierce the center with a pencil and spin the disc; a definite glow of orange will result. Try drawing a simple still life using the dot or pointillism technique; again a small sheet of paper is sufficient. Only then can one imagine the tedious hours it took to complete Seurat's famous painting titled "Sunday Afternoon on the Island of La Grande Jatte." It has been stated this masterpiece took four years for completion. Try drawing a simple still life of objects or fruits you can draw easily and experiment with color combinations, using separate dabs of bright spectral colors (Fig. 8-6A).

Fig. 8-6A: Another style of impressionism, "pointillism"—developed by Georges Seurat.

lesson 7

Cubism

Procedure:

Cubism is defined as an intellectual rather than an emotional form of art. It involves many principles—disintegration of subject; reorganization of subject into colorful, textured and decorative composition; multiplicity of viewpoints; a transparent quality. Georges Braque was the most consistent artist in this style. Other well-known names are Pablo Picasso and Lionel Feinenger, after whom the illustration in Fig. 8-7A was styled.

**Fig. 8-7A: Cubism—an intellectual expression
as opposed to emotional impressionism.**

lesson 8

Expressionism

Procedure:

One definition of expressionism is: "any kind of art in which the personal emotions of the artist are expressed." These artists often distorted nature in their effort for individual self-expression, often leading away from beauty, which did not concern them. Famous names are El Greco (1545–1614) and Van Gogh (1853–1890). A second group of expressionists, formed in Munich, Germany, and called "The Blue Rider," included such names as Nolde, Marc, Kandinsky, and others familiar to art-lovers. Kandinsky, who referred to his style of painting as "color music," was the first artist to exhibit truly abstract paintings without recognizable objects, frequently titling his work simply "Composition." Splashy colors and dark forms in swirling shapes distinguish his style (Fig. 8-8A).

Fig. 8-8A: Expressionistic painting in the style of Kandinsky.

chapter nine

Exploring Combinations of Mixed Media

Introduction

The objective of mixed media lessons is to explore the interaction of media, utilize left-over materials, discover effective combinations and create unusual and original pictures. Through experience and understanding of media characteristics pupils can eventually select their own combinations, beginning with their favorite materials. Watercolor, for example, in its transparent technique gives depth to a picture when combined with opaque tempera applied to foreground areas, producing ariel (atmospheric) perspective.

Mixed media can include more than two materials, such as a trio of Conté crayon, watercolor and acrylic, actually developing into a series of continuing lessons, depending on the age group. The classroom teacher could gradually accumulate items for a special mixed media box in which could be put scraps of colored paper and tissue, broken Payons, crayon shavings in individual small containers, and almost any left-over material ideally suited to combining materials. This is not only a great saver on art supplies but also encourages pupils to pre-plan and think out ideas, challenging them to use their imaginations in finding uses for left-over material.

Many professional artists use mixed media for textural effects, contrast, depth, interaction and originality. Mixed media also offers appealing variety of techniques and freedom of self-expression for all age groups.

lesson 1

Wax Paper and Crayon
with Hot Iron

Procedure:

This lesson is ideal for small groups. Cover the work area with thick pads of newspaper. Place a household iron on a support near a plug for easy contact and removal. On 4″ × 6″ white paper draw a sailboat, usually a popular theme (Fig. 9-1A). Cut a sheet of wax paper the same size and place it directly over the drawing. Heat the iron so it is fairly hot (Fig. 9-1B), press over the wax sheet and immediately trace the sailboat. The heat will assist the crayon to glide smoothly over the drawing, producing rich thick black lines. For colorful pictures use a variety of bright crayons.

Due to the small size of wax paper, the work of many pupils can be displayed at the same time as window transparencies; simply secure them to the glass with invisible tape (Fig. 9-1C). A variety of themes can be developed, related to the curriculum, field trips or seasonal ideas. While the iron is in use cut foil to small sizes, run the hot iron over it and draw subjects from memory,

Fig. 9-1A: Sailboat done with wax paper, crayon, and hot iron.

Fig. 9-1B: Using a hot iron to press wax paper over a drawing.

such as a horse's head (Fig. 9-1D). On cold white paper draw in pencil a plant motif, then redraw in it crayon, and finally iron it in up and down strokes, slightly melting the crayon and creating an interesting textural effect on the total picture (Fig. 9-1E). A watercolor wash can be applied over the entire subject or color can be applied in certain areas of the pupil's choice.

Fig. 9-1C: Securing wax paper drawing to window.

Fig. 9-1D: Drawing from memory—horse's head on hot foil.

Fig. 9-1E: Plant motif created by pressing a crayon drawing with a hot iron.

lesson 2

Conté Crayon and Payons

Procedure:

In chapter 7, notching Conté crayon is explained and illustrated. It is most effective in drawing nature subjects, like a butterfly. Draw this insect (preferably a short one) with a notched Conté crayon on white paper (Fig. 9-2A). Frame it with a broad dark Payon stroke, adding radiation lines at each corner in a sunburst fashion. Dip a brush in water and cover the entire background, leaving the butterfly itself dry. Notice the immediate action of dry Payon changing into brilliant colors (Fig. 9-2B). Now reverse the process, designing the insect and brushing water over it, leaving the background dry and white. Experiment in a variety of applications for your own creativity.

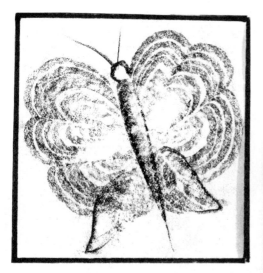

Fig. 9-2A. Butterfly drawn with notched short Conté crayon.

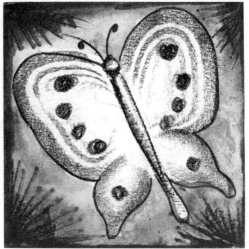

Fig. 9-2B: Background of Payon brushed with water.

lesson 3

Laminated Crayon Abstracts

Procedure:

The art of lamination (in which things are bonded together or built up in layers) can now be explored since the student is familiar with the hot iron techniques. In preparation for such a lesson, especially with younger groups, the teacher could save time and confusion by collecting crayon shavings ahead of time. These could be placed in small plastic containers with covers for convenient storage.

The first experiment is one in pure abstraction. The only guideline for colorful results is to keep the colors apart, because when melted crayons run together they mix into a brown tone, losing the brilliant color contrasts. Let the pupil discover this for himself by making small laminated sheets. Start with a sheet of 9″ × 12″ wax paper folded in half; open and place crayon shavings in individual color groups on the right side (Fig. 9-3A). Fold the left side over and press with a hot iron (Fig. 9-3B). Watch the crayon melt into abstract designs, and stop ironing when a pattern pleases you.

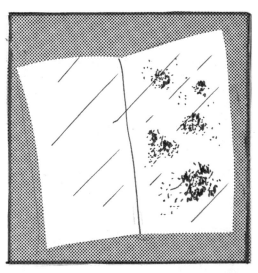

Fig. 9-3A: Place groups of crayon shavings on right half of folded wax paper.

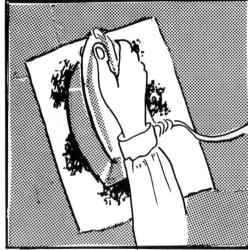

Fig. 9-3B: Fold left side of wax paper over shavings and press with hot iron.

An unusually beautiful lamination is the combination of green pieces of tissue cut into leaf shapes, crayon shavings, and a flattened three-leaf clover. Arrange these in a balanced composition on the right side of a sheet of wax paper (Fig. 9-3C), then fold and proceed to iron until the two sheets are bonded together. This produces a beautiful window transparency. The different shades of green tissue paper create depth, while the crayon melted shavings used in small amounts make solid areas. This idea also makes excellent mobiles, suspended from wire forms and moving in the air current.

Fig. 9-3C: Balanced composition of tissue
leaves, crayon shavings and a
real three-leaf clover.

lesson 4

White Tissue, Black Paper and White Silhouettes

Procedure:

Black paper is a pleasant change from the traditional white background. Mix a solution of one-third water soluble glue (Elmer's) and two-thirds water in a plastic container. Tear bits of white tissue paper into abstract shapes; have too many rather than not enough. Keep the picture area small, 4″ × 6″ with an inch border; when the technique is understood, experiment with larger areas. Brush the glue solution over the entire area within the border, then immediately place the white tissue scraps at random, overlapping some pieces, and brush it again with the solution. In some places it will wrinkle, which is ideal for textural effects. Let it dry. This black background with white accents lends itself to a night scene. Draw a lighthouse, rocks, and crescent moon on white construction paper; cut it out and glue it on the background to make a pleasing composition (Fig. 9-4A).

Now experiment with colored tissue on white paper. This time when scraps are placed on the wet solution crush them with the end of the paint brush handle or your fingers. Next mix a puddle of watercolor, and while the background is still wet run a wash at the top of the paper; hold the paper at a slant so the wash will run down, creating a network of lines and accidental images. Let this dry, then turn the paper in different positions, letting your imagination suggest other subjects. Here a landscape seemed to come into focus; it can be accented with a marker, or other medium of your choice—crayon, ink, etc. (Fig. 9-4B).

Fig. 9-4A: White tissue on black paper, with white cutouts of lighthouse, rocks and crescent moon.

Fig. 9-4B: Landscape made by crushing colored tissue on white paper and accenting with a marker.

lesson 5

Fingerpaint, Tempera
and Cutouts

Procedure:

The technique of fingerpaint is explored in chapter 2 where emphasis is placed on stiff hand positions for best results. Undersea themes are beautifully suited for fingerpaint since both fish and ocean floor plant life (Fig. 9-5A) are easily created with the side of the hand, finger tips and nails. The picture in Fig. 9-5A was executed with black fingerpaint with areas of contrasting sharp white paper showing through, to which, when dry, colorful cutouts were glued in place for a three-dimensional effect.

With a little experience colored fingerpaints can be introduced and developed into a two-lesson project. After the preliminary preparation of the paper is made, paint a blue sky with broad, sweeping hand strokes, and create white clouds, either with the hand or with tissue. Where tree foliage is planned remove most of the blue, leaving enough to resemble sky glimpsed through the trees (Fig. 9-5B). Add a little yellow to the blue fingerpaint and lay in the green

Fig. 9-5A: Underwater scene in fingerpaint, with fish and plants cut out and added.

Fig. 9-5B: Fingerpaint landscape, with paint removed to indicate clouds.

foreground; this is better than using green fingerpaint since mixing blue and yellow produces a varied green similar to nature's colors. Place dabs of yellow and red on the tree foliage areas; when these are mixed with the fingers they produce orange, so the orange fingerpaint is also eliminated.

The second lesson can be devoted to cutouts representing tree trunk, branches, farmhouse, fence, and silo (Fig. 9-5C).

An effective display would be one depicting the four seasons, using fingerpaint and cutouts. These pictures could be set aside and displayed during the year according to the season, eventually giving all the class a chance to exhibit their work.

Fig. 9-5C: A farm scene, including cutouts
of trees, farmhouse, fence and silo.

lesson 6

Payons and Crayons
on Fabric

Procedure:

While Payons are delightful to work with on paper, they are especially exciting on wet fabric—and become permanent when washed. Try the paper technique first on white paper. Draw a border within which a winter landscape is lightly penciled. Dip a brush in water and wet the sky, distant trees, and stream. Leave part of the paper untouched to give the effect of snow. Apply the Payons directly on the wet surface and notice how quickly rich, brilliant tones are produced with practically no pressure. Add blue, green and brown to the stream, leaving horizontal streaks of white paper to create sparkle to the water (Fig. 9-6A).

Before making pictures on wet fabric, explore the procedure of drawing on dripping wet fabric and on damp fabric; the material that is too wet will blur the design as the Payon pigment is absorbed into the cloth. (Test this theory yourself for your own information and better teaching.) Now draw a simple basket on white paper; cut a piece of old clean sheeting the same size as the paper; wet it and wring out until just damp; spread with outward movements of both hands (Fig. 9-6B) over the basket drawing, which will show through the

Fig. 9-6A: Winter scene done with Payons on white paper.

Fig. 9-6B: Spread damp cloth outward with both hands to remove wrinkles.

cloth (Fig. 9-6C). Try a portrait from imagination, using the side of broken Payons. Long hair is laid in with broad strokes, easily and realistically (Fig. 9-6D).

Fig. 9-6C: Place drawing underneath basket; drawing is seen through wet material.

Fig. 9-6D: Use the side of broken Payons for large masses, such as long hair in a portrait.

lesson 7

"Stained Glass" Transparencies

Procedure:

"Stained glass" transparent technique offers a lesson that features freedom, creative expression and fun, resulting in colorful transparent windows and brilliant mobile displays. Use 9″ × 12″ white drawing paper and with a black crayon draw bold dark lines swirling over the paper, first in one direction, then the other (Fig. 9-7A). Prepare six puddles of tempera color: red, yellow, blue, green, orange, violet (no brown or black). Paint the open spaces in solid colors, leaving white paper around each color. Let this first step dry (Fig. 9-7B). Fill in the roads between colors with black crayon, making them all the same width and keeping neat edges (Fig. 9-7C). Into a small plastic dish pour inexpensive cooking oil; then apply it over the entire paper with a flat house brush. Have plenty of newspaper under the artwork, as this helps to absorb the excess oil (Fig. 9-7D).

Since stained glass suggests the Christmas season, cut out an ornament, tree, wreath and bell (Fig. 9-7E). The stained glass technique can also be

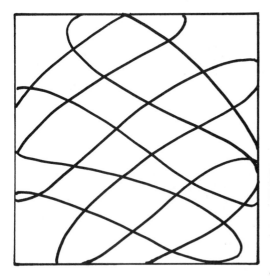

Fig. 9-7A: Free swirling lines create a variety of spaces.

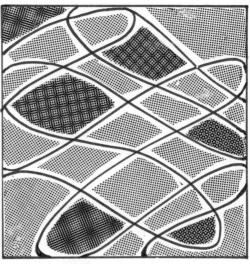

Fig. 9-7B: Spaces filled with color, leaving white paper between spaces.

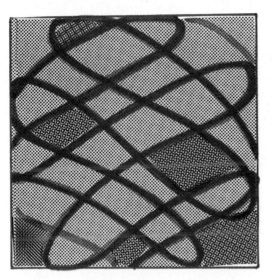

Fig. 9-7C: When colors have dried, paint the white "roads" with black tempera.

applied to colorful mobiles or stabiles. Round decorative angel fishes in different sizes can be cut, threaded and balanced on curved wire to move and dangle in the air currents (Fig. 9-7F).

Fig. 9-7D: Brush over dried tempera with cooking oil.

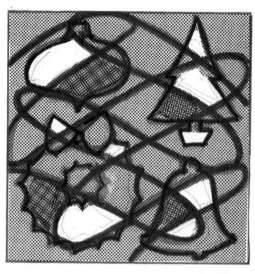

Fig. 9-7E: Place ornament designs under dried transparent "stained glass"; outline with marker and cut out.

Fig. 9-7F: Mobile motifs made of "stained glass."

lesson 8

Crayon Rubbing and Three-Dimensional Letters

Procedure:

The art activity of crayon rubbing is always popular, and is an excellent way to make use of broken crayons; simply remove the paper wrappings and set them aside for this lesson. Here is also an opportunity to review drawing and cutting block letters on folded paper.

There are 11 letters in the alphabet that can be cut this way: A,H,I,M,O,T,U,V,W,X,Y. Two letters are selected for this experiment, "H" and "T." Construction paper weight is good for rubbing techniques, especially if the top paper is thinner. Fold a 4″ × 6″ sheet of construction paper in half. Keeping the fold on the left side, halfway down draw in from the fold a one-inch horizontal bar; on the cut edges draw a one-inch vertical strip. For easy cutting, shade with pencil the part to be removed (Fig. 9-8A). When parts are cut out, open to find a well-proportioned letter "H." The Letter "T" is also drawn on folded paper. Be sure the stem of the letter is drawn half the width (½″) so when the paper is opened it will measure one inch total.

Place these letters under a sheet of white paper in pleasing arrangement.

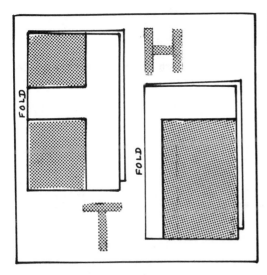

Fig. 9-8A: Using folded paper to make the letters "H" and "T."

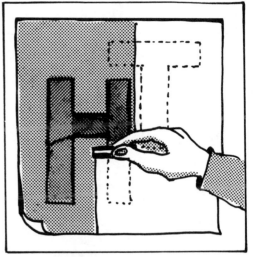

Fig. 9-8B: Using cutout letters for crayon rubbing.

Using the side of the crayon, bear down and pull the crayon toward you with firm downward strokes. The letters will begin to appear as if by magic (Fig. 9-8B). Remove these letters and with tempera paint color the edges a bright gold, silver or bright color. Let dry. Trim the crayon rubbing and mount on contrasting construction paper.

Around a pencil, roll short pieces of masking tape into short cylinders with sticky side out and adhere to the backs of the letters (Fig. 9-8C). Place these a little below and to the right of the rubbed letters; this will make the letters stand away about ½″ from the background, causing a shadow for a three-dimensional look (Fig. 9-8D). This is an extremely dramatic effect for posters and titles.

Fig. 9-8C: Use of masking tape cylinders for three-dimensional effect.

Fig. 9-8D: Fasten cutout letters to the right of rubbed letters to give shadow effect.

lesson 9

Easy Triple Media Class Mural

Materials:

Blue construction paper (9″ × 12″); white chalk, yellow and green tempera paint; bright yellow 3″ squares of construction paper; white or pale yellow 3″ crepe paper squares; tape and stapler.

Procedure:

Art projects involving the total class create enthusiasm and often lead to increased interest in art lessons. A mural can include artwork by all the children, regardless of their talent, resulting in a composite representing the entire class. This activity features a variety of materials, and can be divided into two lessons. The mural illustrated in this lesson is correlated with literature, for its theme was inspired by William Wordsworth's lines:

> I wandered lonely as a cloud
> That floats on high o'er vales and hills,
> When all at once I saw a crowd,
> A host, of golden daffodils.

Daffodils make an ideal theme for this lesson, the objective of which is to join a series of children's drawings in a continuous picture. This is accomplished by using the first lesson to establish an unbroken line of hills. Each child receives a 9″ × 12″ sheet of blue paper, which he holds the wide, or horizontal, way in front of him. Illustrate on the blackboard how to place a dot on each short edge of the construction paper, making sure the dots match; begin with the first seat of each row across the room—usually five rows (Fig. 9-9A). The reason for using blue construction paper is threefold: it is a change from the usual white paper; it eliminates blue paint, since the paper itself represents the sky; it offers an opportunity to use white chalk for a fluffy white cloud. Small containers of green paint should be ready for painting the hills (Fig. 9-9B).

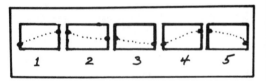

Fig. 9-9A: The first row across the room matches dots on edges of their papers.

Fig. 9-9B: One section of mural, showing chalk cloud on blue construction paper sky.

While this step is drying, a discussion of near and far perspective could be introduced: how flowers look far away (smaller); nearer to the viewer (larger). Photographs of daffodils in a field will help to illustrate this point. When the green paint has dried place small dots of bright yellow paint on the rolling hills, making them a little larger nearer the lower edge of paper. The lesson could be interrupted at this point and continued on another day.

It would simplify the flower-making process to pre-cut 3″ pieces of white or pale yellow crepe paper, 3″ squares of yellow construction paper, and 4″ strips of green paper (use two shades for added contrast). To make the trumpet shown in Fig. 9-9C, hold the grain of the crepe paper parallel to the finger and lightly wind it around the finger, taping the seam. A short piece of invisible tape is excellent for this. For convenience, tear off short strips of tape and fasten one end to the side of each desk. Flute the top edge of the crepe paper by pressing it with both thumbs, pressing in opposite directions to create a ruffled edge. Compass-drawn circles are not necessary in making petals; simply dot each center edge of the 3″ pieces of white and yellow crepe paper and draw an arc connecting the dots. Cut five petals, cutting not too near the center, then push a pencil point through to make a hole. Crush the unruffled edge and force into the center; tape and bend part on back of the petals. Make two or three daffodils; an older group could make graded sizes. Secure these flowers to the lower part of the background, one a little higher than the other (Fig. 9-9D). Take the first row drawings and tack them onto the bulletin board. The hills

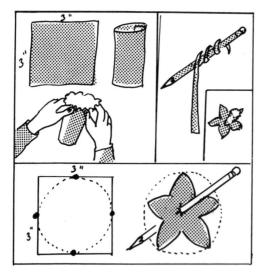

Fig. 9-9C: Making the trumpet petals and leaves.

Fig. 9-9D: Stapling the daffodils onto background.

will make one long continuous line and form a colorful border for the class-room (Fig. 9-9E). Leaves are stapled or taped in front and between the flowers; stems are not needed.

If an older group is making the mural, unusual arrangements can be created. For example, 12″ × 18″ pastel colored paper could be held vertically in random or contour style, with the main line running through the papers (Fig. 9-9F). Smaller 9″ × 12″ sheets of black and white alternating in up and down style could involve the technique of counterchange, with white chalk or paint on the black paper and black paint or marker on the white paper. This would offer a challenge to an older group.

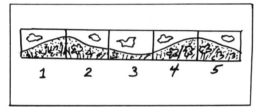

Fig. 9-9E: The finished first row drawings joined together for mural.

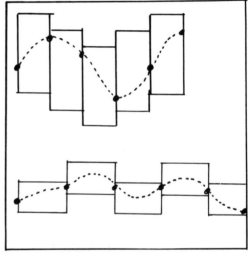

Fig. 9-9F: Unusual arrangements of murals with continuous lines but irregular edges.

chapter ten

Constructing with Easy-to-Cut Cardboard

Introduction

Making interesting three-dimensional forms out of lightweight cardboard is good experience for children and adults alike. Your class will enjoy discovering how transforming flat paper into round shapes creates volume-producing positive and negative spaces. The positive space is tha actual paper cut out, while the negative space is the open part in between. It is the well-organized combination of these two that makes artistic construction.

Oaktag is a lightweight cardboard popular in the classroom. It has a smooth hard finish, and comes in five colors—blue, orange, pink, yellow and green. Oaktag is manufactured in three sizes: 9″ × 12″; 12″ × 18″ and 18″ × 24″. Such items as masks, posters, dioramas, mobiles, hats and abstract constructions can be created in oaktag. Another free material that works well with oaktag is the cardboard tube found in paper towels. Children can bring these in from home and set them aside for art lessons.

lesson 1

Windmill Mobile

Procedure:

Windmills are usually made from square sheets of paper. When your class makes a large one, to prevent waste use 9″ × 12″ oaktag, which produces a slightly different proportion. Have the class choose a striking combination of colors, since the resulting windmill will be a colorful room display.

Begin with a sheet of oaktag, drawing lines from each corner and marking them A, B, C and D. Place a dot one inch away from the intersection, and make a circle 2″ in diameter (Fig. 10-1A). Fold corner "A" to the dot and tape

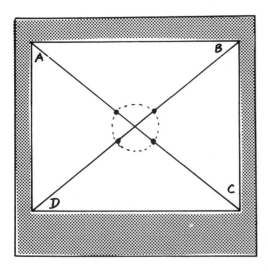

Fig. 10-1A: Draw diagonal lines from corner to corner, and place dots on lines one inch from center.

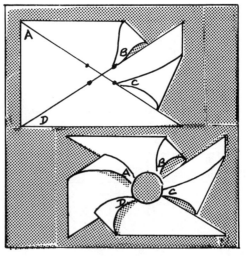

Fig. 10-1B: (1) Fold corners in to the dots and tape down. (2) For added support cut out a 2″ circle and glue over points.

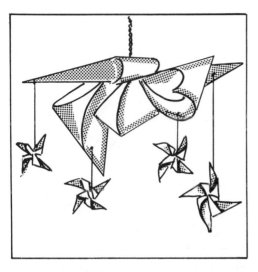

Fig. 10-1C: Mobile made of five windmills.

in place. Do the same to each corner, adding a two-inch circle glued down over the points for added strength (Fig. 10-1B). Next pierce two small holes in the center of the circle, ½" apart, and pull a string through, leaving enough length for it to hang freely. When you have completed the large one, make four smaller windmills of different colors, using square sheets of paper ranging from 4" to 2". Attach them to the wings of the large windmill at different levels. These will move in the air currents since they are hung in a vertical position (Fig. 10-1C).

lesson 2

Owl Mask

Procedure:

A dramatic owl mask can be made from two sheets of bright yellow oaktag. Hold one sheet of the paper horizontally, drawing diagonal lines from each corner. Measure four inches down from corners "A" and "B" and place a dot, then cut to this point. The owl eyes are round and should measure about 1½" in diameter, leaving one inch between the eyes—approximately the same distance as in the human head. To cut holes for the eyes, first pierce the center

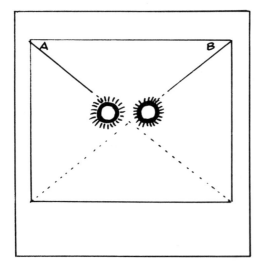

Fig. 10-2A: Draw diagonal lines from corners "A" and "B". Draw round eyes 1½" in diameter.

Fig. 10-2B: Roll beak over pencil; curve lower edge of mask.

of each, then cut to the edge of the circle. This leaves a clean circle. With a black marker or crayon draw a band around the eyes, adding radiating lines outside the border to represent small feathers (Fig. 10-2A). A mouth is not needed on this mask, but the nose is important. Draw an oval 1½" long, color it bright orange, cut around the lower part and roll the beak over a pencil (Fig. 10-2B). By bending the mask, curving the lower part of it, you can make the ears stand out effectively.

Use the other sheet of yellow paper for two foreheads (if there are 20 pupils in the class, only ten sheets are needed). Again draw diagonals (Fig. 10-2C); cut on the lines, saving sections 1 and 2; mark letter "A" on each point; give one to your neighbor; and save the two remaining scraps for the collage box. (Every classroom usually has a collage box in which all sorts of scraps are collected). Roll the center "A" over a pencil. Attach this forehead to the mask so it hangs slightly over the eyes for an owlish look. This part can be glued or stapled. Strings are added to hold the mask on the head (Fig. 10-2D)—and the owl is ready to hoot!

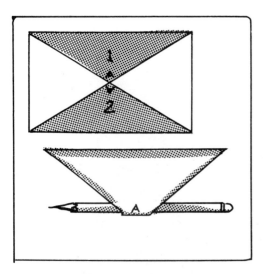

Fig. 10-2C: Making forehead for the owl mask.

Fig. 10-2D: Completed owl mask. Add strings to tie.

lesson 3

Multicolored Strip Hat

Procedure:

The five colors of oaktag are ideal for making a multicolored strip hat. This is a basic hat that can be further enriched with rings, crayon or marker designs, or fringe. The hat is extremely simple to make. Just place a ruler at the top of the paper and draw a line on the other edge, repeating this until the oaktag is filled with horizontal lines, then cut all the strips (Fig. 10-3A). The number of strips you make will depend on the width of the ruler. Join two strips by overlapping an inch and fit it around the head for size. (Two pupils can work together fitting each other.) Secure three strips inside the band with tape, and make a small ring for the top (Fig. 10-3B). To make this lesson a community activity give each pupil a different color, then let them exchange colored strips.

Fig. 10-3A: Making strips for multicolored hat.

Fig. 10-3B: Multicolored hat completed.

lesson 4

Kinetic Autumn Tree

Procedure:

Kinetic means "of or resulting from motion," and in this lesson a tree with moving leaves is created. This particular tree is designed for an autumn theme; however, it can be an all-season tree, with snowflakes, spring buds, or full summer leaves. This can also be a community project in which children learn to work together sharing ideas. Select several strong branches bearing many smaller branches to create a well-formed tree. For the flower pot any containers can be used; cardboard paint bucket, small grocery box, plastic flower pot or container. Place stones inside to weight it down and fill it with soil, inserting the branch securely. If plaster of Paris is available, use it to fill the container, placing the branch in the center and supporting it in a vertical position until the plaster has set.

To make the foliage draw several sets of irregular shapes, large, medium and small, in red, orange and green (Fig. 10-4A). The simplest way to secure the foliage to the branches is to pierce the center of each leaf with a pencil point, cut in from the edge to the center, then spread the cut open slightly and place it over the branch. Use a dab of Plasticine on each side for support. Add the second and third leaves one inch or less apart. Attach these triple sets to the

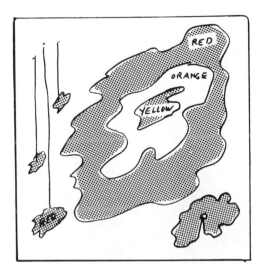

Fig. 10-4A: Kinetic autumn tree in the making.

Fig. 10-4B: Completed tree with falling leaves.

branches until a colorful tree is created. Finally, use dark thread to suspend hanging leaves which will move in the air currents like falling autumn leaves (Fig. 10-4B).

lesson 5

Twin Bunny Basket

Procedure:

Paper can be folded and cut into basket shapes to fit many occasions. In this lesson twin rabbits make an amusing basket. This lesson could first be practiced on construction paper, then on 9″ × 12″ oaktag. Fold the paper in half, then fold the lower section to the center fold (Fig. 10-5A). Place the paper on a hard flat surface and press from the center out. (Do not hold paper in the air and try to make a clean edge.) Cut to the fold, as accurately as possible for sharp corners, at points A, B, C, D (Fig. 10-5B). Fold up the sides by stapling or gluing; add a handle. Cut four long oval ears; cut whiskers from scraps of

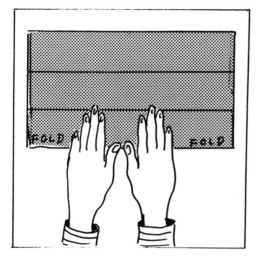

Fig. 10-5A: Fold paper on lines by pressing outward with both hands.

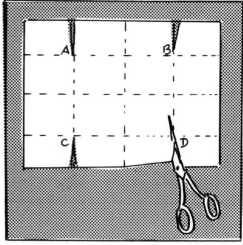

Fig. 10-5B: Make four cuts exactly to fold at points A, B, C, D.

paper; glue them in place; add eyes and nose with crayon or marker. The basket is ready for cookies, candies, or a small gift (Fig. 10-5C). For variety, try different animal heads.

Fig. 10-5C: Twin bunny basket completed.

lesson 6

Giant Birthday Card

Procedure:

Fold a 12″ × 18″ sheet of oaktag in half, placing both hands together at the center and pressing outward—but always matching the corners for equal division. If desired, the teacher can use a marker to write, in big letters, "Happy Birthday, Jane," and further down on the vertical card, "7 years old." Before any decorations are glued on ask the class to come to the front of the room one by one and sign their names on the inside of the card. Then cut up drinking straws into 2″ lengths, run a series of seven strips of glue where the straws are to go, and let the birthday child glue her candles in place. Different children can help cut out small flowers to make the card colorful (Fig. 10-6A). The teacher's name and the date of the birthday should be added. To make the card stand up, glue or staple a support of folded oaktag on the back.

Fig. 10-6A: Giant birthday card.

lesson 7

Small Tom-Tom Drums

Procedure:

One and a half sheets of oaktag will make a small tom-tom drum. These can be decorated with markers or crayons, making a colorful assortment of drums on which to gently beat out rhythms. Cut a 9″ × 12″ piece in half lengthwise, and roll the paper into a cylinder shape to soften it (Fig. 10-7A). If it is to be decorated open it flat and apply the designs, then roll it, overlapping about an inch, and tape, glue or staple. Stand the cylinder on a sheet of paper and trace around it (Fig. 10-7B). Draw another circle about a half-inch wider than the first one and draw radiating lines. Cut on these lines to the first circle, then fold the tabs up. Make two of these circles (Fig. 10-7C), and place one on each end of the cylinder, taping the tabs down. Add another strip over the tabs for a neater finish. The class is now ready to decorate their tom-toms and beat out sounds to music (Fig. 10-7D).

Fig. 10-7A: Fold paper lengthwise and cut on dotted line. Roll paper into a cylinder to soften it.

Fig. 10-7B: Trace around cylinder, then draw another circle one inch away from the first one. Draw tab marks.

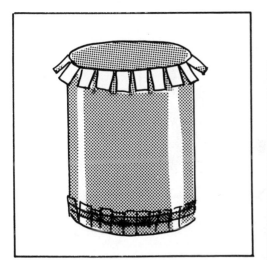

Fig. 10-7C: Fold tabs down and place on top of cylinder. Add base. After tabs are glued on, tape around the cylinder.

Fig. 10-7D: Finished tom-tom.

lesson 8

Abstract 3-D Construction

Procedure:

Negative and positive spaces in three-dimensional projects can create a really artistic work if these are considered while composing the construction. Positive spaces are the actual paper cutouts themselves, while negative spaces refer to the open areas between the cutouts. On 9″ × 12″ oaktag draw freeform shapes, beginning with a graceful swirl design; continue to make other shapes—triangle, circles, and crescent forms. Combine these in a pleasing composition. Make a base to support these shapes and start to build, turning the project around frequently to find different angles. When the construction in Fig. 10-8A was partly composed it looked like the universe, so a star was added. Leave the abstract in colored oaktag or spray it gold.

Fig. 10-8A: Abstract freeform, in the making
and complete.

lesson 9

"Summer Camping" Story Illustration

Procedure:

An appropriate color for a camping scene is green oaktag. Use a 12″ × 18″ sheet folded in half horizontally. Add a flap to the back for support so it will stand easily. Set this aside until the props are made.

Different shades of green construction paper are excellent for the pine trees. Cut four 3″ × 4″ pieces of two shades of green; fold two (of the same shade) in half and cut on the edges to form pine branches. Then staple them together in the center, and spread out the branches to make a full pine tree. Now do the same thing with the second shade of green. For an older group the four sheets can be cut at the same time, then stapled (Fig. 10-9A). Make different sizes of trees.

Make tents by folding paper into triangle shapes, or design your own. Small broken branches create a realistic campfire.

Paint or crayon the backdrop, adding blue sky, purple mountains, rolling hills—whatever fits your idea of an ideal camp site. This can become another class project in which children work together illustrating a story (Fig. 10-9B).

Fig. 10-9A: Cutout illustrations for "Summer Camping" story.

Fig. 10-9B: Camping scene featuring three-dimensional trees and tents.

lesson 10

Cardboard Tube Centerpiece

Procedure:

Cardboard tubes from paper towels make excellent centerpieces; the proportions are ideal, the material strong and clean. Two tubes are fine for one centerpiece. Leave one the original 11″ length; cut the other in half; glue these three together for the base. Decide on the size of your candles and cut holes for easy fitting (Fig. 10-10A). Spray the set with gold quick-drying enamel. Insert foil baking cups into the holes and add the candles. Finally cut oak leaves from colored paper and simply insert in the ends of the tubes (Fig. 10-10B).

Fig. 10-10A: Base for cardboard tube centerpiece.

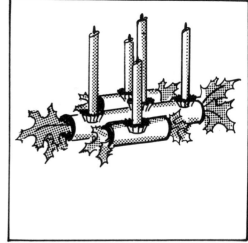

Fig. 10-10B: Completed centerpiece.

chapter eleven
Creating Fabric
Flowers, Collages and Gifts

Introduction

Fabric is an excellent medium for classroom projects, especially if the school has a Home Economics Department; if it doesn't, children can bring in scraps from home, neighbors and friends. It is a perfect medium for exploring textures: smooth, rough, shiny, dull, prints, plaids, stripes, and solid colors. There are professional artists who use fabric in landscape collages, interpreting nature in fabrics; for example, blue satin for water, brown corduroy or rough tweeds for tree bark. Working with fabrics is a totally different experience for both students and adults, not only in picture-making but in making craft items as well. All kinds of projects can be enjoyed—frames, wall hangings, tote bags, masks, standup animals, desk caddies, change purses and many others.

lesson 1

Box Frames

Procedure:

Two frames can be made from a shallow stationery box—one from the base and one from the cover. To find the center of the box, draw two diagonal lines across the top; where the lines intersect is the center (Fig. 11-1A). Mark off the size desired for the picture.

There are two ways to proceed from this point. (1) An older (high school) group can cut out an opening, slightly smaller than the picture that is to be used, with a matte knife, and then cut fabric to fit the base of the box and glue it on smoothly. The picture is then taped to the back of the frame so that it is centered in the opening. (2) A younger group can simply cut material to fit the inside of the box, cut it out and glue it in place. The picture can then be trimmed, mounted on white paper showing a ¼" border, and centered on the fabric. In either case, selecting the fabric to harmonize with the theme and color of the painting is good experience in self-expression. Pierce small holes in the corners of the box frame and fasten string for hanging (Fig. 11-1B).

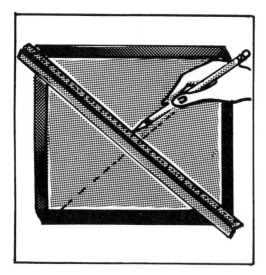

Fig. 11-1A: Making a box frame. A shallow 7" × 8½" stationery box was used here.

Fig. 11-1B: Completed box frame, with picture mounted.

lesson 2

Pictorial Collages

Procedure:

For the first picture select a theme that offers opportunity for contrasting textures; Fig. 11-2A with a lighthouse, water and rocks illustrates this idea. Collect scraps of fabric: blue satin, darker dull blue and greens for water; white for lighthouse and clouds; grey, brown and black prints for rocks; black scraps for accents.

There are two ways to approach picture-making with fabrics: (1) Make a drawing, select the fabric and cut out each element separately. In composing the picture, arrange the fabric pieces so they abut. To create a slightly three-dimensional feeling, cut the sky in one piece and glue it down; add the white cloud next, and last the lighthouse, pressing each section thoroughly. (2) A dramatic but simple approach is to plan a bright-colored still life of fruits. Study the combination of colors you have chosen for the picture, then for background select paper of a color that complements the theme. A pineapple can be cut from dull orange fabric, with narrow strips of brown glued onto it in lattice effect, and dots made in the centers of the diamond shapes with a waterproof marker. Grapes made of purple satin are effective. Add pieces of darker fabric to represent shadows on the fruit. This makes a striking wall display for the autumn months (Fig. 11-2B).

Fig. 11-2A: Lighthouse collage, made of fabric scraps.

Fig. 11-2B: A still life of fruits offers a challenge in selecting fabrics.

lesson 3

Flat Puppets
(for 3-D or Mural)

Procedure:

A puppet drawn on 9″ × 12″ oaktag is a good size to work on, and a good weight on which to paste fabric. For younger children not confident in drawing, a pattern could be made for the use of the entire class (Fig. 11-3A). The final touches added by the children will make each puppet unique. Before actual work on cutting and pasting begins, select flesh-color material for skin, and other material for clothing. Then cut and glue, working on the face and hands first, then adding clothes in your own choice of colors and textures. Bend the puppet at the joints for interesting positions (Fig. 11-3B). These puppets can be used in a mural mounted on brown kraft paper, perhaps depicting familiar community figures—a policeman, a storekeeper, a Boy Scout and a Girl Scout, a doctor and a nurse.

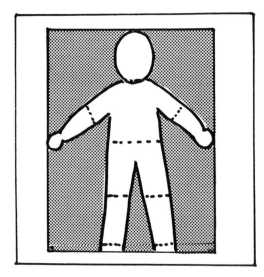

Fig. 11-3A: Flat puppets to be covered
with fabric.

Fig. 11-3B: Bend where dotted lines
indicate joints.

lesson 4

Fabric Banners

Procedure:

Tell the class to think up one- or two-word slogans for a fabric banner. "Hello" and "Smile" make excellent slogans for banners (Fig. 11-4A). For "Smile," have the children decide on the various nationalities they would like to present on the banner, selecting the skin colors and characteristic features of those countries. The teacher can cut and prepare the cloth for the banner, turning over the top edge to make a casing for a length of dowel, to which string is attached for hanging. Then the children can cut out the paper faces, glue on fabric to represent skin, and finally add features and hair. Big letters, SMILE, are added in the center. The HELLO banner in the illustration is made of 18″ × 24″ oaktag or brown kraft paper, using fabric only for the design.

Fig. 11-4A: Fabric banners.

lesson 5

Tote Bag

Procedure:

A fabric version of the brown paper lunch bag, measuring 5″ × 10¾″, is a convenient size and makes a handy gift. A smooth, closely woven fabric (preferably cotton) in a colorful pattern has two advantages: it has eye appeal, and any errors will not be seen too readily. A bright, lively design can be drawn around the summer theme of sailboat, cloud, bird, buoy and water. Simply place the closed paper bag on the material, trace around it and cut. There are five sections: front, back, two sides, and base (Fig. 11-5A). Press each section before gluing to the matching paper section. Finally fold the bag in half at the top and cut a handle (Fig. 11-5B). An older group could add bright-colored "Mystik" tape to the edges for strength and contrast. An initial added with tape personalizes the gift.

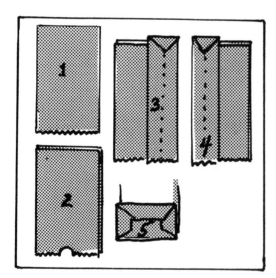

Fig. 11-5A: Brown paper bag used as backing for fabric tote bag.

Fig. 11-5B: Glue selected fabric onto bag; bind edges with contrasting tape.

lesson 6

Bandana Mask

Procedure:

A bandana mask is made by cutting in half, diagonally, a 20″ or 24″ square of old sheeting or material brought in from home. Features are added with fabric scraps. Tie the bandana around the head to establish location of eyes, nose, and mouth. Cut out eyes, a curved slit for the nose, and a mouth the size you want (Fig. 11-6A). Plan an almond-eyed Oriental face, fringing the lower part of the mask for a beard, or a man from Mars with rectangular eyes and mouth, or a flowered face. The bandana mask can be inverted so it becomes a half-mask with a head covering—comfortable, original, and inexpensive.

Fig. 11-6A: Making a bandana mask.

lesson 7

Standup Leopard

Procedure:

Left-over scraps of fabric in a leopard print can be used to make a realistic standup leopard. First of all, provide clear photographs of leopards for your pupils to observe, discuss, and practice drawing. Then make a pattern by folding a 9″ × 12″ piece of construction paper in half lengthwise. Sketch a leopard to fit the size of the folded paper, drawing his back along the fold (Fig. 11-7A). Cut the pattern out, cutting along the fold line as well. (This produces two leopards, so will provide patterns for two students.) Next fold a piece of orange 9″ × 12″ oaktag in half and repeat the process, but this time do not cut the two leopards apart. Place the opened-up pattern on the leopard-print cloth, trace it, cut it out, glue the cloth to the pattern and press. When it is dry, fold it along the crease line, staple the two parts together at the head and at the tail, and your leopard is ready to stand up. Make a background with real twigs and stones (Fig. 11-7B).

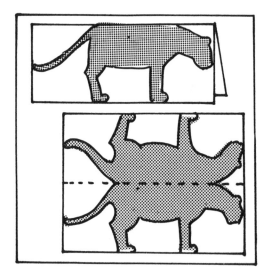

Fig. 11-7A: Pattern for making standup leopard.

Fig. 11-7B: Completed leopard—also shown in appropriate setting.

lesson 8

Handy Table Caddy

Procedure:

Cardboard tubes found in paper towel rolls are clean and strong—perfect material for table caddies, which can be used to hold pencils, brushes, knitting needles, rulers and pens. Decide on several sizes of tubes, and select a shallow, tray-shaped box to hold them neatly. Cover the tubes with fabric in various colors and patterns. To fasten each tube securely to the box, crush ¼ newspaper sheet into a ball, apply glue inside the lower part of the tube (Fig. 11-8A), insert the paper ball, add more glue to the bottom of the crushed paper, stand the tube in the box and press down on it for a few moments. Do the same to all the tubes. Add a bright ribbon and bow to the box, especially if it is to be used as a gift (Fig. 11-8B).

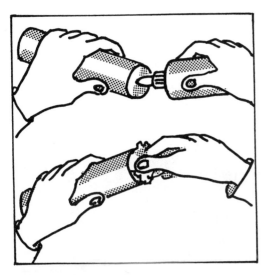

Fig. 11-8A: Making a caddy for desk or work table.

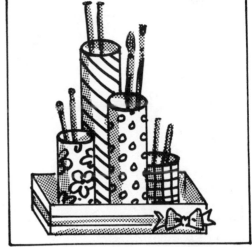

Fig. 11-8B: Completed caddy.

lesson 9

Budding Fabric Branches

Procedure:

Budding fabric branches make a bright and colorful spring display in the classroom. Select well-formed branches the length you need for a particular display. Choose a fabric with a small bright print or plain colors, in two shades, so some buds are light pink, for example, and others darker rose. Cut 3" squares, fold in quarters, and round off the corner; when opened, a circle is created. Grasp the center with the fingers, twisting it into a bud appearance, and tape it to the end of a branch. Repeat this on all branches, adding leaves if you wish (Fig. 11-9A). The rosebud, dogwood and poppy are also easy to make and quite realistic if done in an appropriate fabric. The rosebud is a 3" × 9" strip of cloth rolled tight at first and then gathered loosely and tied with wire, string or tape. The dogwood is a square, folded in quarters, and shaped into four petals. A button can be used for the center, a pipe cleaner threaded through for a stem. The poppy center is a circle stuffed with crushed newspaper surrounded with a strip of cut petals; a pipe cleaner is also used to hold the flower together and produce a stem (Fig. 11-9B). Red taffeta with a black center makes a dramatic poppy.

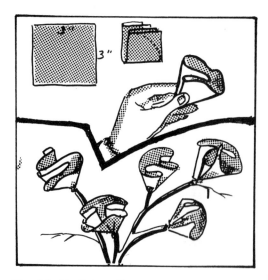

Fig. 11-9A: Fabric flowers on real branches.

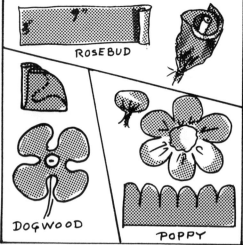

Fig. 11-9B: Cloth rosebud, dogwood, poppy.

lesson 10

The Envelope Purse

Procedure:

It is not necessary to design a pattern for an evenlope purse; a 3″ × 6½″ white stationery envelope is perfect. Carefully open it flat, marking a letter "A" at the top point of the stick-down flap. Place the pattern on a piece of polka-dot material, pressed smooth, and trace around it. This step can be omitted for a younger group; just cover the paper pattern with glue and press it onto the cloth, keep it on wax paper under weights until dry, and then trim it. Repeat this step, gluing the cutout pattern with the polka-dot covering onto contrasting fabric (in this case a striped one), pressing and cutting it out (Fig. 11-10A). Sew a button on the lower flap, staple a short strip of elastic, tied in the middle, to the upper flap; lower loop goes around the button. Add a bright-colored or black initial. The gift is now ready for admiration and use (Fig. 11-10B).

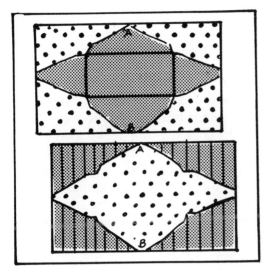

Fig. 11-10A: Making an envelope purse.

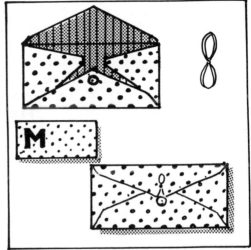

Fig. 11-10B: Envelope purse completed.

chapter twelve

Designing with Paper (Opaque and Transparent)

Introduction

One of the most useful and least expensive materials for art projects is newspaper. Not only is newspaper vital for covering work tables, it can also be used by your girls and boys to produce many creative, useful and decorative items. Newspaper is easy to cut, fold, crush and paste. It provides an excellent background to paint and print on, especially the even grey tones of the financial sections. You can teach your class to work with many other opaque papers, including construction paper (double colored and single), foil, brown kraft or grocery sacks, crepe paper and opaque white plastic bags. They can also make things of transparent material, including wax paper, clear plastic, saran wrap, tissue and cellophane. All these materials are available at newsstands and supermarkets. Projects such as flowers, greeting cards, seed starters, masks, headdresses, hand puppets, small kites, booklets and many more can be made from paper, in activities both adults and children can enjoy.

lesson 1

Clear Plastic Flower

Procedure:

Small clear plastic bags, commonly used for sandwiches, are available at the supermarkets. These can be transformed into unusual flowers by a small addition of colored construction paper. Since each package usually contains 100 bags, measuring 6¾" × 8½", and 100 twists, a class of 30 pupils can each make three blossoms, resulting in a galaxy of colorful flowers for classroom decoration or gifts to take home.

Each pupil can make a flower first by cutting a strip of construction paper into 4" × 9", or the teacher can precut these strips in multicolors. The pupil should fringe one side of the strip down about 3", roll it around a pencil and tape the end. Notice what a graceful form this rolled paper creates (Fig. 12-1A). Hold the sandwich bag at an angle and insert your hand, stretching your index finger into the corner. Place this over the fringed center and twist the bag around the stem. Some air will remain in the bag, making it puff out. These blooms can be attached singly to a straight branch, in pussywillow formation, alternating down the stem, or attached on various branches for a colorful display.

Fig. 12-1A: Making a flower from a clear
plastic bag.

lesson 2

Wax Paper Flower

Procedure:

Wax paper combined with crepe paper is another effective bloom. Cut out a 4″ square (or any size you wish), and fold in quarters. Next cut off the open corners, making a curve; open to find a circle. Cut into the center, making a small hole; cut three of these. It is better to cut each one separately since wax paper slips. Overlap and tape to form a cup shape; repeat on all three. For the center use a 4″ × 4″ strip of crepe paper; roll around a pencil, keeping grain parallel with the pencil. Holding each end of the crepe paper push hands together, crushing the paper; remove from pencil, unwind gently and rewind into a bud shape. Insert into the three wax cups and tape in place. To add delicacy and color contrast, fringe a 4″ × 4″ piece of green construction paper and place it around the stem, wrapping it tightly with pieces of green crepe paper for strength (Fig. 12-2A).

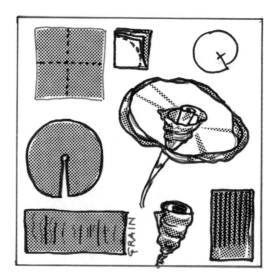

Fig. 12-2A: Making a flower by combining
wax paper and crepe paper.

lesson 3

Reverse Flower

Procedure:

Cut a strip of crepe paper 6″ long and 4″ deep on the grain; fold in half and then in thirds; shape the top in a pointed oval, open and stretch the center of each petal with your thumbs to create a cup effect. Make the center of the flower out of a piece of wax paper 12″ long (the width of the roll) by 4″; the teacher could have these all torn off and ready for the class. Fold the 12″ wax paper in half, and then in half again, resulting in a 4″ × 3″ rectangle. Fringe the two short sides and gather together with a pipe cleaner; twist, making the fringe fan out. Wrap the strip of petals around this stem; tie with twist tie or tape; cover with green crepe paper (Fig. 12-3A).

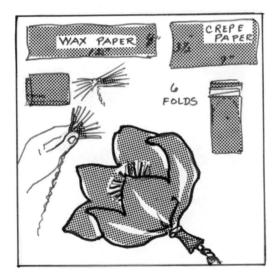

Fig. 12-3A: Flower made by combining wax paper and crepe paper in reverse.

lesson 4

Butterfly Clip

Procedure:

The clip clothespin makes a good base for an ornamental butterfly, fish, or bird; almost any theme can be used. Double-colored construction paper is more expensive but due to the small amount required it is ideal here. Plan the size of butterfly you want for the first experiment on plain construction paper or newspaper, then use the good paper. A clip clothespin measures 3¼″ by ½″; the paper size required would be 3¼″ × 6″. Fold in half and again in two more folds so the center strip can be glued onto the clothespin (Fig. 12-4A). This could develop into a science study discussing color, designs, habitat, sizes, in relation to geography. Use crayons, markers, or paint to record the design of a specific butterfly or have fun making your own fantasy markings. Clip the finished butterflies to branches, curtains, or bulletin boards.

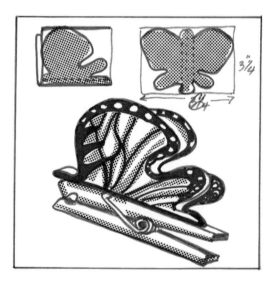

Fig. 12-4A: Butterfly clip made of double-colored construction paper.

lesson 5

Embossed Foil Greeting Card

Procedure:

Working with foil is a worthwhile activity, especially if it is a small-scale project to begin with; this saves on foil and introduces the material to the pupils. It is also an excellent way to make use of stray envelopes with no matching stationery. Decide on the final size of the card you plan to design, making it at least ⅛" smaller than the envelope for easy insertion. If a heavier piece of cardboard is used, a single sheet is enough; however if a French fold is preferred, use the pattern to make four sections, folding it into fourths (Fig. 12-5A). A ''Happy Birthday'' card is always popular. Cut a circle of cloth or flat cotton batting and glue it onto the center of the card; then place a piece of smooth foil over the card, leaving a small border. With the end of a pencil, letter the message on the foil, and press it down around the face to raise the circle. Make lines or dots for added design. This technique is called embossing. Draw a smiling face for the receiver to enjoy.

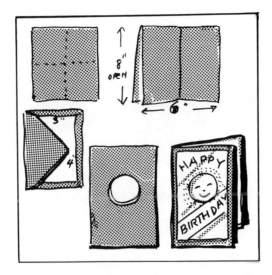

Fig. 12-5A: Embossed foil greeting card.

lesson 6

Foil Seed Starter

Procedure:

Collect different sizes of small cans; let children select their own or invite them to bring some in from home. Tear off strips of foil big enough to circle the can and bend under for a strong base. Wrap it around the tin can—not too tightly; then fold the excess under the tin, smoothing it carefully. Remove the container to find a short foil cylinder (Fig. 12-6A). Fill the seed starter with soil and bean seeds, water it, and watch the little beans start on their way. If a strip of masking tape is wanted on the foil, be sure to attach it while on the tin can, pressing it firmly in place and lettering it before removing the can.

Fig. 12-6A: Foil seed starter.

lesson 7

Lion Mask or Wall Plaque

Procedure:

Select a sheet of 12″ × 18″ tan construction paper; divide it lightly in fourths to help in drawing a face. Draw an oval that touches all four sides (Fig. 12-7A). Here is another lesson where research and discussion help motivate the class and assist the pupils in drawing the animal. The eyes are well above the center line and are close together; the nose is long, broad and flat; the jaw appears to be made up of three circles. In the upper right and left corners cut two 3″ circles for the ears. Clip them to the center, overlay and staple them, and glue them to the head (Fig. 12-7B). Cut out the eyes, under the nose and up slightly on the sides. It isn't necessary to open the mouth unless the student prefers it that way.

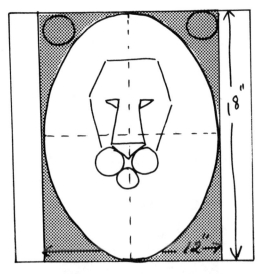

Fig. 12-7A: Beginning step in making lion mask or wall plaque.

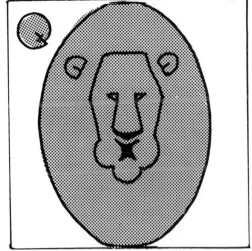

Fig. 12-7B: Making and attaching the ears.

The next step makes the mask dramatic and unusually realistic. Use three sheets of 9″ × 12″construction paper, yellow, orange and brown, drawing horizontal lines about ½″ wide across the papers. Roll four strips at a time around the pencil halfway down (Fig. 12-7C). When all the strips are curled begin to add to the head, curling them over the forehead in front of the ears, and continuing until the head has a full mane. Tie on strings for the mask wearer's use; simply tuck the strings in back when the mask is used for a wall plaque (Fig. 12-7D).

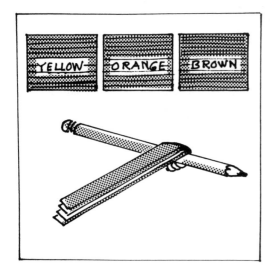

Fig. 12-7C: Making fur for the lion mask.

Fig. 12-7D: Completed lion mask.

lesson 8

Elaborate Indian Chief Headdress (Newspaper)

Procedure:

Expense in making such an elaborate Indian headdress is of little concern since newspaper is the material used. Open a double-page sheet flat, fold in half, and glue together with wallpaper paste. Repeat this step with another folded sheet so there will be four layers (Fig. 12-8A). This is an expandable headdress, made of as many feathers as wanted. Fold this long strip up 2″ along the bottom, staple or glue in place, then begin planning the feathers, starting with the center one. A three-inch width is a good proportion. While the strip is flat paint the feathers first; when dry cut the points and the sides of the feathers. Make an added strip down the back as long as desired; place around the head for size, and staple. Add fluffed-out bits of cotton batting above headband. Study pictures of Indian headdresses for variety in design and color (Fig. 12-8B).

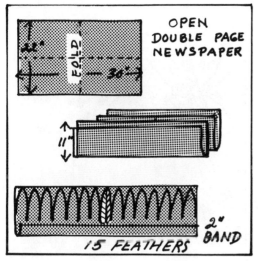

Fig. 12-8A: Making feathers for an Indian headdress.

Fig. 12-8B: Completed headdress.

lesson 9

Plastic Bag "Rufus" Hand Puppet

Procedure:

The opaque white plastic bags, 17″ × 18″, found at the supermarkets are excellent for hand puppets since the bag is long enough to adequately cover the arm. These come 30 bags to a package so one box is sufficient for a class. The bags are cut in half and glued, or tape can be used; however, tape will be more expensive. To make the dog head crush half of a single sheet of newspaper into a ball, poking the index finger in it to make a hole for finger manipulation (Fig. 12-9A). Place this ball in the bag, pulling out the corners for ears. Keep the index finger in the head and let another classmate tie a pipecleaner around the neck just tight enough to allow the finger to wiggle. With a permanent black marker add features on the head (Fig. 12-9B).

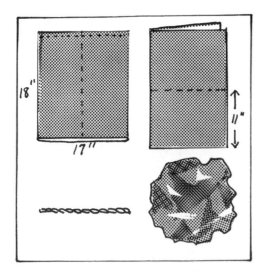

Fig. 12-9A: Making a hand puppet from a plastic bag.

Fig. 12-9B: "Rufus"—completed hand puppet.

lesson 10

Mini-Kites

Procedure:

Making small kites serves many purposes—an art lesson, fun at recess, and party favors. It also encourages creativeness in designing different kinds. One sheet of oaktag will make two kites—first, one from the original design, then one with left-over scraps. Fold a 9″ × 12″ sheet in half and cut, making two 6″ × 9″ pieces. Fold one 6″ × 9″ sheet in half lengthwise. Draw a distorted diamond shape (Fig. 12-10A). Be sure you draw from the fold, then cut out the shaded areas neatly so the scrap pieces can also be used. Open, and glue a center strip in place, as shown in the illustration. Place a sheet of bright-colored tissue over the kite and glue in place, trimming off excess tissue. Fold the other 6″ × 9″ sheet in half, following the same procedure, and glue that kite over the tissue. Add strings and small butterfly tissue bits to the tail.

To make the "scrap" kite, glue the longer triangle over the shorter one, press, fold in half and cut out the shaded areas, then follow same steps as before (Fig. 12-10B).

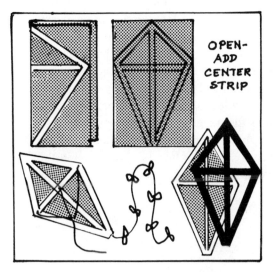

Fig. 12-10A: Mini-kite made of oaktag and tissue.

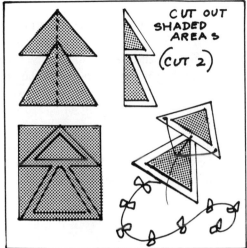

Fig. 12-10B: Mini-kite made of left-over scraps.

chapter thirteen

Using Paper Bags for Party and Everyday Items

Introduction

The resourceful teacher will make it a practice to collect paper bags for creative craft lessons. Paper bags come in a variety of colors, styles and sizes, challenging inventiveness and imagination. Useful and decorative projects can be made, and children enjoy bringing a paper bag to school only to return with it transformed into an animal, fish or bird. The most versatile bags are the brown lunch bag and the large grocery sack; once a project is made with the lunch bag it can be copied in the larger size. These bags are easy to cut, and accept paint and crayons quite well. Wrinkled bags need not be discarded; dampening and ironing while hot restores the material to almost new. Interesting creative ideas can be made: animals, birds, parade shakers, chains, miniature tables, hand puppets, masks, and many others. Once bags are used in the classroom, individual projects will develop—especially with children who like to invent and explore.

lesson 1

Fish Hand Puppet

Procedure:

This hand puppet can also be used as part of a mobile, suspended to swim in the air currents. To motivate the class display a colorful fish completely finished, and illustrate how to manipulate it by opening and closing the base with the fingers inside. A helpful suggestion is to exhibit brightly colored pictures of various types of fish, either to be copied or as an inspiration for a fantasy fish design. Keeping the bag closed and flat, paint the top and underside, then open the base, painting this part bright red for the mouth. With a black marker spread the side of the bag flat, making a large eye on each side (Fig. 13-1A). Add scales and gills for dramatic and realistic effect.

The second bag is used for the tail and fins. First cut off the base of the bag and save for another lesson, then fringe the entire remainder, open, and cut off a few strips for the side fins. A classmate can help on the next phase by closing the bag on the puppeteer's arm just enough for easy insertion, then taking it off and stapling it. Finally glue the fringe around the opening, add fins, and the fish is ready to perform (Fig. 13-1B). With the hand inside, simply open and close the mouth, showing the bright red interior.

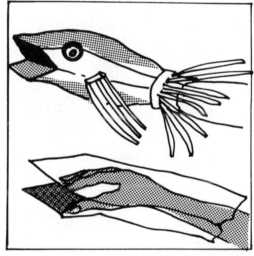

Fig. 13-1A: Fish hand puppet made of a paper bag.

Fig. 13-1B: Fish hand puppet completed.

lesson 2

Exotic Birds

Procedure:

These lessons are devoted to fringing since so many interesting things can be made with fringe. A good rule to follow is *always color before cutting*. Place the bag with the folded base up. Folding the open end to the base, draw a dotted line, cut and fringe to this line. Keeping it flat, fold it lengthwise, drawing the bird's head on the base part (Fig. 13-2A). Open to find two birds; separate them and color the head, eyes and beak on both sides. Puff out one bird, twisting a tie around the body and spreading out an exotic tail. Do the same to the other bird, then tape them onto branch, facing each other (Fig. 13-2B).

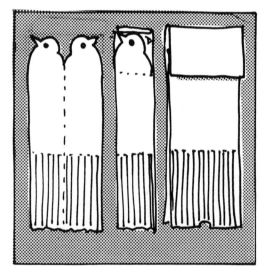

Fig. 13-2A: A paper bag makes two exotic birds.

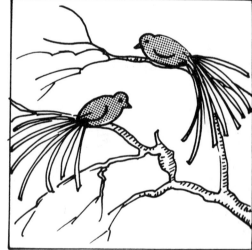

Fig. 13-2B: Exotic birds sitting on branches.

lesson 3

Palm Tree

Procedure:

Place a bag folded and flat on the table; cut to the base in an evenly spaced fringe; roll around a wide stick, knitting needle or large marker and tape, forming a cylinder. Notice how it fans out into a handsome shape (Fig. 13-3A). Twist another bag, closed, to form a tree trunk and insert it into the palm tree cylinder. It may need a little glue on the end before inserting. Since bags are inexpensive it is best to make a test one first before coloring it. The easiest way to apply color is to open the bag, place it on a full branch to keep it in position, and spray with quick-drying green enamel paint. The trunk needs only a few streaks of brown paint to give it a realistic look. Plan a background of mountains, water, and clouds, and support the tree with rocks and small bushes (Fig. 13-3B) for a typical Hawaiian scene.

Fig. 13-3A: Making a palm tree for Hawaiian scene.

Fig. 13-3B: Hawaiian scene completed.

lesson 4

Parade Shaker

Procedure:

Two paper bags per pupil will make a shaker used in school yard parades or to keep time to music in the classroom. It is so easy, especially since the palm tree lesson has already been used. Make two palm tree foliage tops and insert one into the cylinder of the first; tape in place. Again spray with bright colors first, let dry, then proceed to make the shaker (Fig. 13-4A).

Fig. 13-4A: Parade shaker.

lesson 5

Paper Bag Chains

Procedure:

Keep the bag closed and cut off the end with the half circle (point X in Fig. 13-5A) to make both sides even. There are two ways to cut the strips— either in ½″ widths, making a total of 15, or cut freely as many as you wish. (Save the bases for Lessons 6 and 7.) Turn each strip inside out and immediately a beautiful shape results. Tape ''A'' and ''B'' together, continuing this until the desired length is made. If ½″ strips are made it will yield three yards, with the circles closed; however, a festoon style can be used if the chain is hung in a draped fashion. Again, after the pupil is familiar with the procedure plan color combinations and what type of paint to use (Fig. 13-5A).

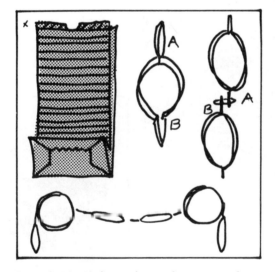

Fig. 13-5A: Making chains from paper bags.

lesson 6

Miniature Paper Bag Table

Procedure:

Cut the base off two bags or use two bases saved from other paper bag lessons. Fold the flap of each base back, as it would be when opened, to form a square base, then staple the bases over each other, leaving the cut edges up (Fig. 13-6A). Glue craft sticks into these open folds, let dry, turn table right side up, and a miniature display area is ready for small items such as sea shells (Fig. 13-6B).

Fig. 13-6A: Making a paper bag table.

Fig. 13-6B: Paper bag table completed.

lesson 7

Individual Aquarium

Procedure:

Fold a closed bag in half and cut an opening above the base, leaving an inch border (Fig. 13-7A). Stand the bag up and open. Fill a clear plastic bag with one cup of sand and place inside brown bag, folding the remainder of the plastic over the top of the open bag. Cut off the base of another paper bag of the same size; design small fish, paint them and cut them out, attach threads to each and suspend from the base, which is then placed over the aquarium (Fig. 13-7B). For colorful classroom display each aquarium tank can be painted a different color, or it can be left in the natural bag color.

Fig. 13-7A: Making a paper bag aquarium.

Fig. 13-7B: Paper bag aquarium completed.

lesson 8

Smiling Tooth Puppet

Procedure:

This puppet is made in the same manner as the fish hand puppet except that an opening is cut to allow three fingers to show through on the edge, making a smiling tooth face, much to the amusement of the class. Fig. 13-8A illustrates the hand position and Fig. 13-8B the effect of the fingers. A big smile and few strands of yarn complete the fun project.

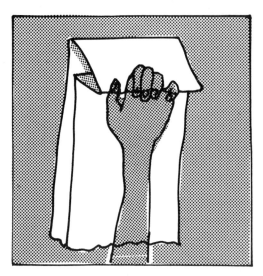

Fig. 13-8A: Making a "Smiling Tooth" puppet.

Fig. 13-8B: "Smiling Tooth" puppet completed.

lesson 9

Mystery Half-Mask

Procedure:

Cut the sides out of a lunch bag (Fig. 13-9A), leaving the front, bottom and back of the bag in a continuous strip. Open the strip flat, place it around the head, and when it fits, staple it. Put it back on the head, covering the eyes. Gently rub a dark crayon on the paper to mark where the eye holes should go. Remove the strip and cut out the eye areas. Shape a curve over the nose. The cutoff pieces (Fig. 13-9B) can be used to make hair. After the lesson is understood, make another mask—this time with a definite color scheme.

Fig. 13-9A: Cutting a lunch bag for use as a half-mask.

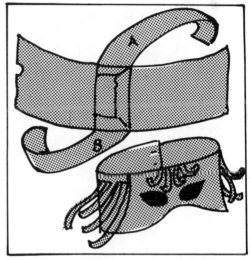

Fig. 13-9B: The finished half-mask.

lesson 10

Creative Blossoms

Procedure:

Fold the open end of bag to the base, and cut on the dotted line (point X on Fig. 13-10A). Save this left-over piece for the flower center. Keeping the bag still closed draw two wide petals; cut and open to find six petals. Open the bag to the square base, pierce a hole, crush the left-over piece into a pointed shape and insert in the hole, then crush the base and center together, securing it with a pipe cleaner (Fig. 13-10B). Wrap green crepe paper around the pipe cleaner for a stem. For color, either spray paint or hand paint, showing veins and other details to enrich the blossom. A multitude of colorful blooms can be made for school plays or corridor or room decorations at little expense.

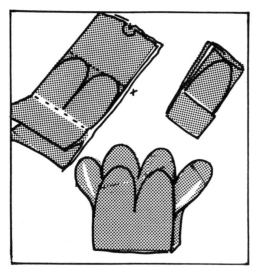

Fig. 13-10A: Making a six-petaled flower.

Fig. 13-10B: Making center for flower.

chapter fourteen

Making Animals from Paper Plates, Straws, and Paper Cups

Introduction

Paper plates, straws and cups offer your girls and boys many opportunities to create animals or birds in different dimensions. Some of these animals can stand alone, and others can be mounted, in relief, on flat pictures, creating a three-dimensional effect. These finished animals can be hand painted or sprayed with quick-drying enamel, then accented with acrylics.

To motivate a lesson in animal construction, display a variety of plates, straws and cups, inviting class discussion as to how these materials can be transformed into birds, penguins, turtles and many more. Fortunately, paper plates and cups come in different sizes. Straws too, are not only straight—some types have a flexible bend. Have pupils draw animals on paper first, to save on the supply of plates. When an idea seems usable then have the pupil proceed to develop the particular subject.

While constructing these animals, your pupils can be motivated to learn more about them. Investigation into the habitat of the penguin, for example, and how it affects his coloring, activity and structure, can result in an informative lesson.

lesson 1

Paper Plate Turtle

Procedure:

The paper plate turtle is easy for the lower grades to make. The material includes two 6″ paper plates and one sheet of brown construction paper (Fig. 14-1A). Cut the 9″ × 12″ paper into quarters. Roll one piece around a large marker for the head and neck; tape while on the support. Staple the end of the nose and clip off corners; it quickly resembles a turtle's head. Cut four feet as illustrated, making one pattern and cutting all four at the same time. The tail is a long narrow triangle. On the first plate, around the rim, staple or tape the head (cut an oval for inserting the neck), feet and tail (Fig. 14-1B). Then add the top plate and staple it in place. Hand paint the turtle's markings, using a yellow-orange for the undershell. Add the eyes with a black marker.

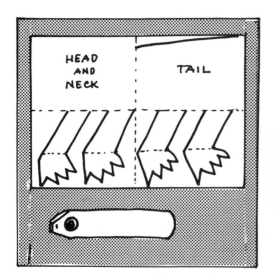

Fig. 14-1A: Pattern for making paper plate turtle.

Fig. 14-1B: Paper plate turtle completed.

lesson 2

A Bluejay

Procedure:

Two 6″ paper plates make this effective bluejay. Fold the first plate in half, using the fold for his back, and tape together at the stomach. The second plate is cut in half; one section becomes the tail, the other is divided to make the head and wing (Fig. 14-2A). Assemble the total bird and hand paint his markings. Place on a real branch (Fig. 14-2B). Other birds can be developed, resulting in a study of birdlife. Many photographs around the room help motivate this type of lesson and at the same time encourage the pupils to become sensitive to the world of nature around them.

Fig. 14-2A: Using a paper plate to make a bluejay.

Fig. 14-2B: Bluejay sitting on a branch.

lesson 3

"Porky" Wall Plaque

Procedure:

This jolly pig only needs two 9″ paper plates and a paper cup. Cut one plate in half, setting one half aside for future animals. Divide the other half; these two pieces form the ears. Simply fold the rim part back, leaving the pointed part for the front of the ears. Staple or tape in place on the second plate. Any cup with a flat base forms the nose; glue it on the face with Duco cement and weight it down for a few minutes. With a black marker add eyes and nostrils. The portrait is now ready for wall display (Fig. 14-3A).

Fig. 14-3A: Pattern for "Porky" wall plaque.

lesson 4

A Jungle Elephant

Procedure:

The elephant is a good project for a slightly older group, and invites an interesting study of the comparison between African and East Indian elephants. The African elephant has exceptionally large ears, the East Indian very small ones and they differ in other characteristics as well. Patterns could be made first on construction paper to save on the plates. However, it might be worthwhile to mention here that you should never discard scraps of plates, straws or cups until the craft lesson is over. Shape the body, cutting two and stapling together, add ears and tusks (Fig. 14-4A). The legs are made by cutting the two cups in half, removing the bottom part and rolling the half cup into a cylinder; then staple or tape. Stuff the legs with newspaper for added strength. When all is assembled spray the elephant with grey paint, add white toenails and tusks with acrylic paint, and make the eye with a black marker (Fig. 14-4B). Stand your elephant alone for display or make a background of the jungle or the open plains of Africa.

Fig. 14-4A: Pattern for making an elephant.

Fig. 14-4B: Completed elephant.

lesson 5

A Performing Seal

Procedure:

All one needs to make a seal is one 9″ paper plate, one 6″ cup, one 2½″ cup and scraps of paper; also a small piece of Play Doh or Plasticine (Fig. 14-5A). Different-sized stones will also add to the final display. Roll the 9″ paper plate so one end is smaller than the other; this makes an excellent tail. Tape the large cup onto the wide cone end and the smaller one on top, tilted back to reflect the characteristic pose of a seal. Add a rounded Plasticine nose, tape the flippers in place, and spray the entire seal with a dark grey paint. Cut fine fringe from scraps of paper and glue on for whiskers. Plan a display table on which the class can show off their seals, adding rocks and stones so the animal will be on different levels. A background painted to show water and distant islands would create a perfect setting (Fig. 14-5B).

Fig. 14-5A: Making a performing seal.

Fig. 14-5B: Seal in realistic setting.

lesson 6

The Country Mouse

Procedure:

The country mouse has such an appealing look that he is sure to amuse and charm the children. Materials are few—two 6″ paper plates and construction paper. To make the head, cut the base off one of the plates; make a cut into the center and overlap, making a convex (forward) shape (Fig. 14-6A). To form the ears, cut two construction paper circles, at least 3″ in diameter. As you did with the plate, cut into the center of these circles and overlap, making a convex shape. Attach ears to the head. A pattern can be used for the body, which is made from the second plate, but instead encourage the children to create their own—a large oval with a long tail. Add whiskers and features. This country mouse is especially appealing on a drawing of a farmhouse and field (Fig. 14-6B).

Fig. 14-6A: Making a country mouse.

Fig. 14-6B: The country mouse completed, shown in appropriate setting.

lesson 7

A Penguin

Procedure:

Only one 6″ paper plate and scraps make this 7″ tall penguin. Fold the plate in half, using the fold for the back. Cut tail, head and flattened wings, and attach these parts. If scraps from other paper plates are used for the tail and feet, your penguin will stand alone. To display penguins in their natural environment, simply cut pieces of Styrofoam and place them around the different penguins the class makes (Fig. 14-7A). This lesson can illustrate a study on these unusual birds.

Fig. 14-7A: Penguin.

lesson 8

An Owl

Procedure:

There are two ways to use this theme: either make just the head for a wall display, or add another plate for the body to make a full bird. Trim the 9″ plate to form a triangle at the top, and fold it over so the point forms the forehead of the owl. Spray or handpaint the head before adding eyes and nose. Use paper baking cups for the eyes; on one, with a black marker, make large black eyes, leaving a white highlight in the black area; glue this cup to a second one which has been spread out a little. Repeat for the other eye. Roll a piece of orange paper to make the bill and glue in place, close to the eyes. It is now ready to mount on the wall (Fig. 14-8A).

To make a full bird just add another plate for the body (Fig. 14-8B). Curl orange paper for the claws and let them rest on a real branch. This is a perfect display for November. The illusion of fine feathers can be made by painting with brown, white and grey, drawing them in their natural growth lines.

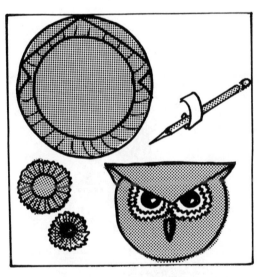

Fig. 14-8A: Pattern for making owl.

Fig. 14-8B: Owl mounted on real branch.

lesson 9

The Ostrich

Procedure:

Straws are excellent to work with; however, for standing birds where extra support is needed, it is best to insert pipecleaners (Fig. 14-9A). The head is made of Play Doh or Plasticine, the body of two 6″ paper plates, and the feet of paper baking cups folded into quarters. The feathers can be real ones, or can be made of folded baking cups or cut out of paper. To assist the bird in standing, prop it against a ''tree''—a branch embedded in a lump of Play Doh. This also lends atmosphere (Fig. 14-9B).

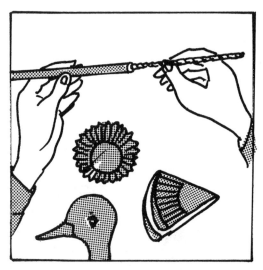

Fig. 14-9A: Steps in making an ostrich.

Fig. 14-9B: The completed ostrich.

lesson 10

The Frog Game

Procedure:

Collect two paper plates, two paper cups, and paper scraps (Fig. 14-10A).

This frog game can be played indoors by taping the rim of the plate to the floor to keep it from moving or outdoors by weighting it down with stones. The objective is to roll a marble through the opening under the mouth. Fold a plate in half, open and paint it red, then reclose, stapling the sides to another plate turned upside down. Tape the scraps of paper, on which large black eyes have been drawn and colored in the center, to the smaller cups; attach these to the top folded plate. Color the frog realistically or leave cups and plates uncolored. If frog is to be painted, use green spray paint before taping on the eyes (Fig. 14-10B).

Fig. 14-10A: Materials needed for frog game.

Fig. 14-10B: Frog game completed.

lesson 11

The Spider Crab

Procedure:

The spider crab, made of two 6″ paper plates and ten plastic drinking straws, looks quite realistic. Plastic straws do not stay in a bent position unless a pipe cleaner is inserted as illustrated in Fig. 14-9A. Photographs in the classroom are helpful in suggestions for color, shape and leg construction. Place one 6″ paper plate face up and tape the legs in position after the basic shape of the shell is made. Then staple the top plate over the lower shell (Fig. 14-11A). Spray the whole crab a dull green and place some of the spider crabs in a box of sand. If desired, a background of beach, surf and distant sand dunes can be added.

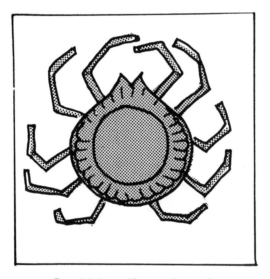

Fig. 14-11A: The spider crab.

chapter fifteen

Hanging and Table Objects of Flat Papier Mache

Introduction

Flat papier mache is made by brushing art paste between layers of newspapers and pressing out smoothly. The number of sheets depends on the particular object—for example, a biplane glider can be made from eight layers of newspaper for strength and durability.

Flat papier mache has many advantages. Since pupils use a brush to apply the paste, their hands do not become sticky. Patterns (creative and printed) can easily be applied to the layered newspapers. Pupils can form objects while the papier mache is still damp or dry, and then spray or hand paint them. Your class can produce interesting projects, including mobiles made of geometric shapes illustrating color theory, decorative and useful fans of many nations, birds, puppets, relief pictures, portfolios and other objects.

lesson 1

The Biplane Glider

Procedure:

When your class is working with newspaper, do not cover the worktable with other newspaper but rather cut open a dark green or brown leaf plastic bag and use this as a cover. This affords desirable contrast while students are working on the project, and the paste will not stick to it as easily as to newspaper.

First, take eight pages of newspaper of the size needed. Place the first sheet on the worktable and brush paste over it (Fig. 15-1A), then immediately cover it with the second sheet.

With both hands flat, press outward, smoothing any wrinkles (Fig. 15-1B). Let dry. Repeat until you have eight layers. Trace patterns as shown in Fig. 15-1C. (Note: In the figure, the wings are reduced; they have to be drawn 5½″ × 1″.) While the flat papier mache is drying, make the wing supports with pipe cleaners, measuring 2″ long; cut eight. Keep the top and bottom pipe cleaners straight; only when the biplane is ready for the wings are the ends bent over the wing edges (Fig. 15-1D).

To attach the lower wing simply fold the body or fuselage in half and cut a narrow slot through which you slide the wing. A slit is needed at the end for the stabilizer and rudder. If the young artist wants a pilot, cut a small figure and

Fig. 15-1A: Applying paste to layers of newspaper to create flat papier mache.

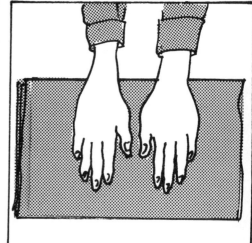

Fig. 15-1B: Pressing out wrinkles.

glue him in the cockpit above the center of the slot. Add the paper clip and the biplane is ready to glide. The plane can be sprayed one color and details handpainted with acrylics.

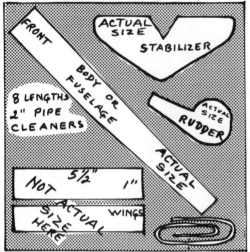

Fig. 15-1C: Pattern for biplane glider.

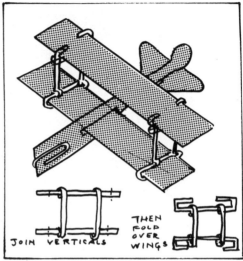

Fig. 15-1D: Completed biplane.

lesson 2

Fans of Different Nations

Procedure:

The study of fans from different nations can develop into a fascinating art lesson, involving various styles, sizes, color and design, and history. Three layers of paper usually make a fan that is easy to fold and staple. Cut paper 7" × 14", pasting the three sheets together as explained for flat papier mache. While this stage is drying is an excellent time to plan the design and edge pattern, scalloped or pointed. When the paper has dried and painted begin the accordion fold, then staple the end. Make a handle with a strip of three layers, place it on either side of the base of fan and paste a strip around for neat finish. The fan can be used in plays, in an oral report on a particular country, as room decoration—and is also a practical item on a hot day (Fig. 15-2A).

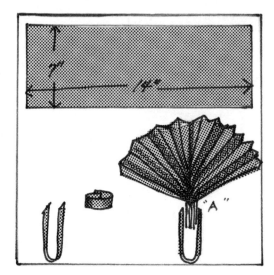

Fig. 15-2A: Making a fan.

lesson 3

The "Sloop" (Sailboat)

Procedure:

Here is an opportunity to make a relief picture illustrating a racing boat with sails billowing. (A relief picture is one in which some of the parts stand out from the background.) The actual pattern is ready for you (Fig. 15-3A). Only three pieces are needed, but they should be made of six layers of paper for support of the relief work. Trace these patterns and transfer to the dried layers. Paint a scene on 9″ × 12″ paper showing blue water, distant islands, clouds and white caps. Shape the hull of the boat so it rounds forward; do this by pasting the bow and stern onto the background. Round out the sails also and glue in place at the top and base. This three-dimensional effect makes a dramatic wall or border display (Fig. 15-3B).

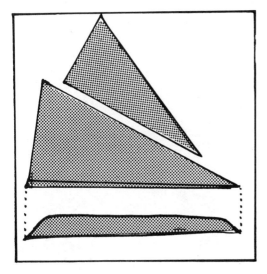

Fig. 15-3A: Making a sloop as part of a relief picture.

Fig. 15-3B: Finished relief picture, showing sloop sailing.

lesson 4

Geometric Mobile (Color Theory)

Procedure:

Studying color theory can be interesting if mobiles are made from flat papier mache. Four layers are ideal since they are easy to cut and the finished product will be lightweight. Draw an 8″ square; fold in half. Beginning at the fold edge, draw a border about 1¼″ wide; cut on the lines (Fig. 15-4A). When opened, the center square will drop out; make this square ¼″ smaller and repeat the first step. There are now three pieces: a small solid square and two larger open squares. Paint each piece, on both sides, one of the three primary colors—red, yellow and blue. Join them with threads, one inside the other, so they will move in the air currents without touching each other. Make another set of three squares (two open and one solid) exactly as above. This time paint them with the secondary colors—orange, green and violet—and hang on the diagonal. Attach both parts of the mobile to a curved wire and suspend by a thread fastened in the center (Fig. 15-4B).

Fig. 15-4A: Starting a geometric mobile.   Fig. 15-4B: Geometric mobile illustrating color theory.

lesson 5

Portfolio

Procedure:

Each pupil can make his own portfolio for special events such as field trips or history or science projects. Start with seven layers of newspaper, which will make a fairly strong cover. When the layers have dried, cut into a 12″ × 18″ sheet, fold in half, and draw a line ¼″ away from the center on each side of the center (Fig. 15-5A). Folding on these lines provides a ½″ spine at the back of the portfolio to accommodate papers that will be placed in it. Make pockets by adding, at the bottom of the left and right sides, layered paper measuring 5″ × 8″. Paste the pockets down on three edges, rounding out the front of each pocket slightly to provide space for inserting papers and envelopes. Plan an attractive color scheme and design an eye-catching title. The portfolios will be useful for displays at PTA meetings and can also be used as gifts (Fig. 15-5B).

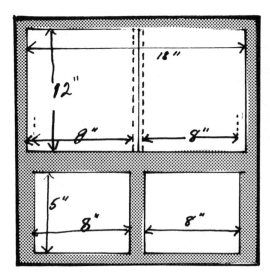

Fig. 15-5A: Making a portfolio.

Fig. 15-5B: Finished portfolio.

lesson 6

Abstract Slab Sculpture

Procedure:

To experiment with abstract slab sculpture begin on a small scale, using six layers of 9″ × 12″ paper. With no attempt at making a picture, just draw three swirling or straight lines that will divide the paper into four shapes (Fig. 15-6A). The pieces can be cut while still slightly damp and shaped into original forms (Fig. 15-6B). Try an arrangement in a horizontal position (Fig. 15-6C). Explore the possibilities of vertical composition, supporting it until dry (Fig. 15-6D). Build this arrangement flat, then stand it up.

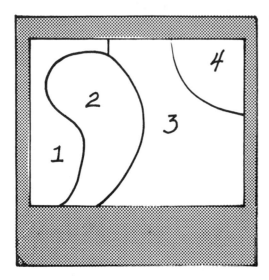

Fig. 15-6A: Dividing the paper for abstract slab sculpture.

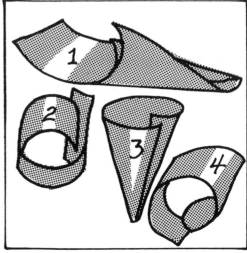

Fig. 15-6B: Final sculpture—curves and cone.

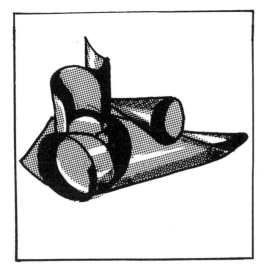

Fig. 15-6C: Horizontal arrangement of slab sculpture.

Fig. 15-6D: Vertical arrangement of slab sculpture.

lesson 7

Hanging Cones
and Cornucopia

Procedure:

Experiment with a small circle first. Cut it in half and overlap the straight edges, making a pleasing cone shape. Tape, staple, or glue. Fasten several together and hang (Fig. 15-7A). It is wise to sketch the idea first, making patterns to be used on flat papier mache. Six-layer papier mache is strong enough for lollipops, candies, or flower arrangements. A single large circle, shaped into a cone and with its pointed end bent slightly, makes a good cornucopia. Fill it with fruit made of Plah-Doh or Plasticine. Play-Doh is excellent for this purpose since it dries white, ready to paint, or can be purchased in colors for most of the fruits (Fig. 15-7B).

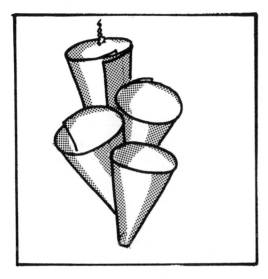

Fig. 15-7A: Hanging cones.

Fig. 15-7B: Cornucopia.

lesson 8

Seagull

Procedure:

Fig. 15-8A shows a pattern for making a 4½″ seagull of four-layered paper. Only four pattern pieces are needed: one wing spread; two bodies; one tail. While the four layers are slightly damp, shape the body, puffing it out to form a round body and gluing it together at the tail and the head. Then add the upper tail and the wing spread. The legs are made of pipe cleaners, inserted into the body. Stand the bird on real stones, or make your own stones by crumpling left-over flat papier mache and pasting it firmly to a stiff board (Fig. 15-8B).

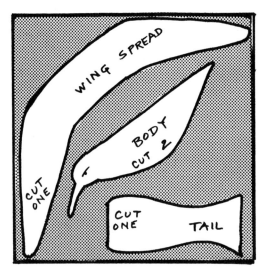

Fig. 15-8A: Pattern for seagull.

Fig. 15-8B: Completed seagull.

lesson 9

7½" Tall Puppet

Procedure:

The purpose of suggesting patterns is to allow the pupil to experience immediately the fun of working with flat papier mache. This puppet measures about 7½" tall when completed. Prepare eight layers of paper, this time letting it dry; then trace the five shapes, adding another arm and leg (Fig. 15-9A). When assembling with thread be sure to reverse one arm so both thumbs are close to the body. The puppet can be painted first, front and back; dried and threaded, he is ready to jump around.

Puppets can be made to represent characters in a story, which the students can act out by manipulating them, using a table as a stage (Fig. 15-9B).

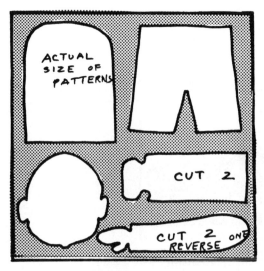

Fig. 15-9A: Pattern for making puppet (actual size).

Fig. 15-9B: Completed puppets.

lesson 10

Handy Memo Holder

Procedure:

Have your pupils sketch an idea for a memo holder, stressing design and color scheme and their importance in decorating. Prepare eight layers of newspaper. When they have dried, fold the strip in half lengthwise and staple onto a coat hanger (Fig. 15-10A). An easy approach to painting is to first spray the 8″ × 11″ strip a bright color on one side and a contrasting color on the other. When dry, apply the design with acrylics. This makes an ideal gift.

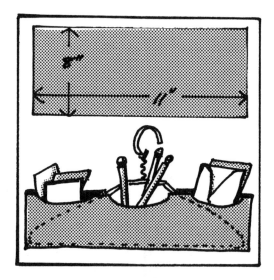

Fig. 15-10A: Handy memo holder with coat
hanger support.

lesson 11

International Flags

Procedure:

Flat papier mache is ideal for making flags. Decide on the size you want and glue them around straws. They can be left stiff or, while slightly damp, curled around a pencil for a waving effect. Three flags are used here—United Kingdom, United States and Canada—inserted in a ball of Plasticine, Plah-Doh or Styrofoam, representing the world (Fig. 11A).

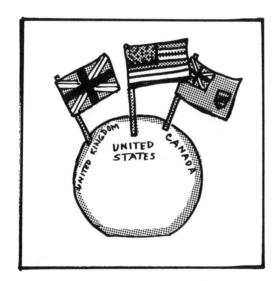

Fig. 15-11A: International flag project—
educational and easy.

lesson 12

Hanging or Table Basket

Procedure:

A good model to use in shaping flat papier mache strips is the 4″ round plastic oleo bowl; two are needed for this lesson. Prepare five layers of paper, cut into one-inch strips, and while still damp fit over the bowl, upside down. Place the strips (four are enough) in a star fashion (see ''A'' in Fig. 15-12A), leaving at least 3″ for handles. Cut strips in fourteen-inch lengths. Wrap a strip just under the rim to hold these pieces in place. To shape the handles invert a second dish, rim to rim, and fit strips over neatly. When totally dry snip the handles, remove the top dish, retape handles together. Spray or hand-paint the basket (Fig. 15-12B). Real drooping vines make this an attractive addition to any room, also a delightful gift. The basket can hold dried flowers or, by leaving a plastic container inside, can be used for real flowers.

Fig. 15-12A: Making a basket to carry or hang.

Fig. 15-12B: A hanging basket.

Chapter sixteen

Making Interesting Things out of _Plastic, Foil and Paper Containers_

The supermarket, where plastic, foil and paper containers adorn the shelves, has long been a haven for art ideas. Rinsed out and dried, these containers have tremendous potential for art projects, either in the classroom, or at home, or in club organizations. A wide range of ideas is possible, including animal cages, masks, bird-feeding stations, music boxes, maracas, flower containers and hanging seasonal decorations. These basic forms provide free materials for creative inventiveness.

lesson 1

Cereal Box Animal Cage

Procedure:

Any cereal box makes an excellent animal cage. Spray it one color, then decorate it with bright designs like those seen on circus wagons. On the piece cut out from one side, draw four wheels and pierce a hole in the center of each. Insert a drinking straw slightly longer than the width of box in each two sets of wheels, forming axles; rest the cage on these two axles. To simulate the iron bars and yet make it possible to change the animals inside, cut two ½″ strips a little longer than the opening and glue in vertical bars, evenly spaced. Secure the top horizontal strip but leave the lower one free to lift up for replacement of wild animals (Fig. 16-1A). The animals are paper cutouts with a support in back so they stand alone.

Fig. 16-1A: Cereal box animal cage.

lesson 2

Egg Box (Six-Eye) Mask

Procedure:

There are many styles of egg boxes but the one with six openings on the cover makes an easy and comfortable mask. Simply cut into the edges halfway across on both sides, and staple the overlapping pieces. Spray the mask with a bright color, decorate, add strings—and the six-eye mask is ready to provide viewing from many angles (Fig. 16-2A).

Fig. 16-2A: Mask made of egg box cover.

lesson 3

Two Styles of Bird Feeding Stations

Procedure:

A quart-size (or half-gallon) milk or juice container makes an excellent bird feeding station; it is strong and waterproof. Before using, rinse it thoroughly with warm soapy water, and let it dry. Glue and staple the top closed. On one side, near the bottom, cut a square or circular opening; insert bird seed. On the front, tie or wire a piece of suet. Push a small branch through the box next to or through the suet for the birds to stand on while eating. Place two more small branches or twigs at the base of the carton, attach a wire with which to hang the carton, and the birds will have a new feeding station (Fig. 16-3A).

To add a roof to the feeder, trace the base of the carton on the center of a paper plate and mark the resultant square into eight sections, as shown in Fig. 16-3B. Cut the sections into eight flaps, and bend them up. Drop the plate over the carton and tape around the flaps to hold the roof in place (Fig. 16-3C). Spray the entire feeder.

Fig. 16-3A: Bird feeding station made
from a milk carton.

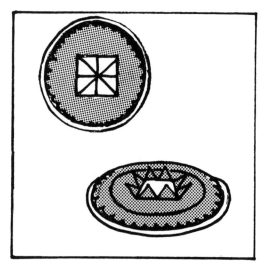

Fig. 16-3B: Making a roof for the feeder.

Another way of making a milk carton feeder is to invert the carton and cut through one corner of it (Fig. 16-3D). The top, glued and stapled closed, now makes a holder for the seed. The carton sides open out to form protective panels for the birds as they sit on their perch (again made of a small branch pushed through the carton sides) and dip into the seed.

Fig. 16-3C: Completed feeder.

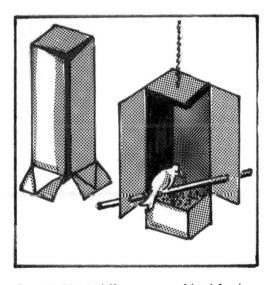

Fig. 16-3D: A different type of bird feeder.

lesson 4

Egg Music Box

Procedure:

Cut the cover off an egg carton and place it under the carton, stapling it securely. Spray the box and let it dry (which it does almost instantly if you use quick-drying spray enamel). This type of box can take only four strings of elastic, since stretched elastic will not hum if it touches or rests upon any part of the box. Use new elastic, cut and tie a knot at each end, and insert in a small cut at the ends of the box (Fig. 16-4A). The box is now ready for a musical treat and is very effective when strummed to music.

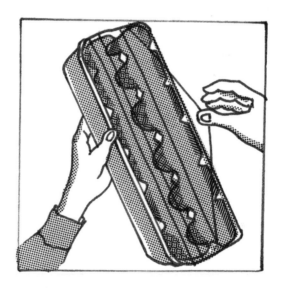

Fig. 16-4A: Egg music box.

lesson 5

Frog Tissue Box Game

Procedure:

Select a tissue box with a wide center opening. There are three ways to decorate the box: cover it with patterned Con-Tact paper, hand paint it, or spray it. Draw a wide mouth, then draw half a circle at the top edge for each eye. Repeat the half-circle on the other side of the fold to make the upper part of the eye; cut the top side and bend it forward; color the pupil black (Fig. 16-5A). Draw circles of heavier cardboard for discs to spin into the mouth. Invent your own scoring system: an easy way to keep score is to have two sets, each a different color.

Fig. 16-5A: Frog tissue box game.

lesson 6

Teaching Clock

Procedure:

Tissue boxes, which are plentiful, make good "clocks"; however, any tall box will do for this lesson. Covered with wood grain Con-Tact paper it makes an impressive time piece. Cut a large circle of white paper, glue it in place on the box and letter the numbers clearly (Fig. 16-6A). Insert a brass paper fastener through black hands, short and long; these hands will be moved to show changes in time so make them of heavier cardboard for durability. If the box is to stand alone, put heavy stones inside to weight it down.

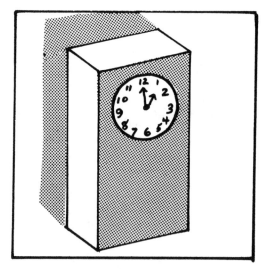

Fig. 16-6A: Teaching clock.

lesson 7

Maraca or Shaker

Procedure:

Rinse a half-pint cream carton thoroughly with warm soapy water. Spray it a solid color, then paint with gay designs. Partially fill with rice or uncooked popcorn. Use a craft stick for the handle, covering the end of the stick with glue and inserting it in the open section. Staple it for added strength, and let it dry before using (Fig. 16-7A). Your maraca will make a loud sound as you keep time with the music.

Fig. 16-7A: Maraca from a cream carton.

lesson 8

Flower Holder
from a Tissue Box

Procedure:

This fresh flower holder, created from a tissue box transformed by means of very little material, makes an attractive centerpiece. Use a tissue box with an oval opening, which will form the pattern for the six large petals. Make the petals of double-colored construction paper which is especially beautiful since the petals will curve upward, showing the contrasting hue. (Some tissue boxes have floral designs with no advertising. They are ready to use—you simply add petals.) At the narrow end of the oval petal make a slit and overlap; glue together. Make six petals, taping them to the under side of the box. Cut the four top opening sections in scallops and bend back. Insert a glass container to hold the cut flowers, and the centerpiece is ready for guests (Fig. 16-8A).

Fig. 16-8A: Flower holder from a tissue box.

lesson 9

Miniature Japanese Garden

Procedure:

The foil TV dinner tray makes a natural container for miniature Japanese gardens. An in-depth study could be made of this distinctive country with its beautifully designed lanterns, Oriental trees, charming bridges over pools surrounded with delicate blooms. To create the pool, use acrylics to paint the largest section in front blue, add water; or cover the rest of the tray with newspaper and spray the water area with quick-drying enamel. Construct a bridge by gluing toothpicks on a strip of construction paper. Fill the remaining three sections with soil and plant selected branches to which green foliage of crumpled or fringed paper has been added. The lantern can be made of Plasticine or Play Doh and painted grey. The foil rim will increase the charm of this individual Japanese garden (Fig. 16-9A). A classroom competition could be encouraged for the most original garden.

Fig. 16-9A: Miniature Japanese garden.

lesson 10

"Please Leave a Note" Door Stopper

Procedure:

Dish detergent plastic bottles have a human shape conducive to the making of cartoon figures. If friends call while you are away, they appreciate finding note paper available so they can tell you they were there. Remove any labels, fill the container with sand, insert pipe cleaner arms at the shoulders and glue a small paper cup on top for a cartoon face. Cut small pieces of paper, rolling them into a short tube at the top to hold a pencil; glue to bottle (Fig. 16-10A).

Fig. 16-10A: "Please leave a note."

lesson 11

All-Season Hanging Decoration

Procedure:

This hanging decoration is best constructed in all white so any seasonal color scheme can be used. Six small 2″ white cups are used, plus six 3″ white pipe cleaners. Slip the cups halfway down "A" and curl each tab around a pencil "B" (Fig. 16-11A). Bend a pipe cleaner in half and insert open ends into the center of the base ("C"); fold the ends flat on the inside ("D"); dip folded end in glue and insert into the Styrofoam ("E"). Attach the six cups around the ball. The illustration shows only one cup cut and curled for less confusion in the drawing; however all six when curled and attached make an ideal "all-season" hanging decoration for Thanksgiving (bright-colored autumn leaves in the Styrofoam, yellow flowers in the cups), Christmas, Valentine's Day, May Day, or even everyday themes (Fig. 16-11B).

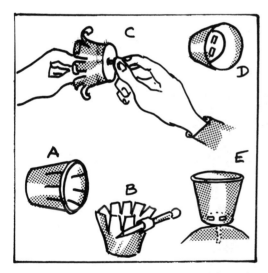

Fig. 16-11A: Making an all-season hanging decoration.

Fig. 16-11B: Hanging decoration completed.

lesson 12

Individual Foil Bells
or Flowers

Procedure:

Individual pie foil dishes are perfect for bells. Just cut from the rim to the center, overlap to the cone shape you like best and staple. Tie yarn around a strip of foil and crush into a ball, thread the yarn through the center, and hang a group of bells from a light or bulletin board (Fig. 16-12A). To make a flower, use a crushed foil center and fringe bright-colored tissue paper into a burst of fluff, secure to heavy chenille green pipe cleaners for a distinctive bouquet. Each flower can have a different colored center.

Fig. 16-12A: Individual foil bells.

lesson 13

Lollipop Centerpiece for Parties

Procedure:

An unbreakable centerpiece can be a welcome feature for a party, whether at home or in the classroom. Select three foil pie plates in progressive sizes. A metal or heavy candle holder with a smooth candle forms middle of the centerpiece. Around the base of the candle attach a lump of Plasticine, and after a small hole has been pierced in the center of the foil dish, press the plate firmly down to hold. Do the same with the remaining two foil dishes, securing the Plasticine under each one. The lollipops, wrapped individually in clear cellophane, are then arranged candy end outward. The three-tiered centerpiece makes a colorful display, and the lollipops can be used as prizes or as a take-home treat at the end of the party (Fig. 16-13A).

Fig. 16-13A: Lollipop centerpiece.

chapter seventeen

Designing Small Creative Gifts in Plaster of Paris

Introduction

Plaster of Paris can be an exciting experience for both children and adults in making small creative gifts. When poured in a creamy state it produces a smooth, snow-white surface that receives paint and ink exceptionally well. It dries quickly, depending on the thickness, and can be made into useful and decorative projects. For successful results preparation should be thoughtfully considered: a worktable covered with plastic sheeting, dark green trash bags cut open, an area for drying where the items will not be disturbed, and all articles necessary for the activity ready at hand. For students with sensitive skin a protective measure is suggested. Pour some hand cream into the palms and coat the hands, letting it dry before working with this medium. Practice on a small scale first, to become acquainted with the characteristics of plaster of Paris. Use non-porous and plastic containers for best results. Remember to tap the container of plaster before pouring, to release air bubbles which will rise to the top. These bubbles are caused by air being stirred into the mixture. Understanding the potentials of the medium will result in successful projects, lessons of fun and enthusiasm.

lesson 1

Abstract Forms Introduction

Procedure:

The most successful way to introduce plaster of Paris activity is to work with small amounts and to concentrate on abstract forms. The objective in this beginning lesson is to learn how to mix this medium and how to pour it, and to understand its drying features and which molds are best to use. Abstract forms can be made from a variety of containers; the non-porous ones are ideal since the plaster does not stick when the container is peeled off. Select five small molds such as a small paper cup, a medium-size cup, half of a plastic egg-shaped nylon holder and a couple of small boxes. To mix the plaster use one cup for the powder, fill a second cup ⅓ full of water. With a plastic spoon, sift the plaster into the water (Fig. 17-1A). Keep adding plaster until a dry island is formed above the water level. Do not stir during the sifting of plaster. When the island begins to appear stir slowly, smoothing out any lumps, until the mixture becomes creamy, not thin. Tap the cup and watch the bubbles rise to the top; air bubbles cause holes in the finished result. Fill the molds at different levels, let set, then peel off the container; a snow-white, smooth surface is produced. Arrange these abstract shapes into a complex form, using your imagination; let it remain white or hand-paint it. Display these abstract forms by placing them on colored construction paper (Fig. 17-1B). Encourage the pupils to give their arrangement a name—museum, hospital, library or school. Try to have every one of the abstract forms an original.

Fig. 17-1A: Sifting plaster of Paris.

Fig. 17-1B: Abstract forms made of plaster of Paris.

lesson 2

Freeform Snapshot Frames

Procedure:

On the prepared worktable add sheets of wax paper to pour plaster on directly. Pour from a 2″ tall paper cup for better control. Mix plaster of Paris a little thicker this time and then pour in a circular shape, leaving an opening in the center like a doughnut (Fig. 17-2A), but in a freer form. Let it set and dry, then lift it off the paper and glue a snapshot in back of the center. The ''Family Album'' (Fig. 17-2B) could be made by gluing each frame on a sheet of heavy dark paper. No two frames will be alike. A simple repeat design border could be painted on the edge.

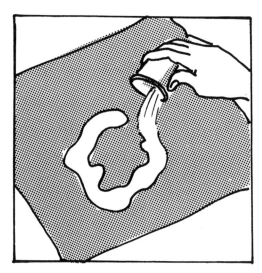

Fig. 17-2A: Pouring plaster into shape of doughnut.

Fig. 17-2B: The Family Album.

lesson 3

Desk Pencil Tray

Procedure:

Select four or five pencils and a shallow box to hold them. If the box cover is not plastic then line it with foil, mix the plaster of Paris, tap the cup before pouring and fill the box. Watch the mixture begin to set and then rub soapy solution around the pencils and embed them ⅓ of the way into the plaster. Let it dry thoroughly, slip out the pencils, decorate the tray and a practical and attractive gift results (Fig. 17-3A). Add a piece of felt underneath so it won't scratch the desk. Another vertical pencil holder is made by pouring plaster into a small plastic dish. While it is setting cut up large straws and embed as many as you wish. Snip a few cuts on the top edges of each straw to help the pencil stay in place (Fig. 17-3B).

Fig. 17-3A: Pencil tray for desk.

Fig. 17-3B: Stand-up pencil holder.

lesson 4

Standing Block Initials

Procedure:

Use the initials of the person who is to receive the gift. Three inches is a good height for the initials. Draw them in block letter style, which means each part of the letter is the same width. Draw the three initials on paper and make a tracing. The letters WBS are used here to illustrate the reverse procedure needed to make the letters come out right (Fig. 17-4A). There are eleven letters in the alphabet that can be reversed without turning the drawing over; A, H, I, M, O, T, U, V, W, X and Y. Roll or smooth out a piece of ½″ Plasticine; turning the tracing paper over, trace each letter on the clay (Fig. 17-4B). Cut out the Plasticine and fill with plaster of Paris, let it set and dry. Remove the mold and stand the letters up, gluing them to a piece of wood or other base. This makes a delightful personal gift. It can be painted in two colors, the front and back the same and the sides a different hue. Instead of initials, MOM, DAD, PTA or others can be used.

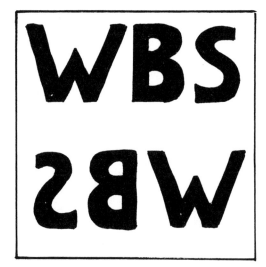

Fig. 17-4A: Standing block initials.

Fig. 17-4B: Block letters used for desk initials.

lesson 5

Easy-to-See
12-Month Calendar

Procedure:

There are many ways to make a 12-month, easy-to-see calendar; here are two. The first is simply to fill a quart milk container (previously soaped and rinsed clean) with plaster of Paris. Let it set and dry, then peel off the carton, glue a calendar on—three months on each side. Add decorations. Before the plaster has set, a looped piece of string can be inserted in the top to resemble a candle (Fig. 17-5A). In the same illustration three cardboard tubes have been rinsed with soapy solution, dried, filled with plaster, and this time finished with four months on each tube.

Fig. 17-5A: Easy to see 12-month calendars.

lesson 6

Everyday and All-Season Hanging Decorations

Procedure:

Plastic cookie cutters are ideal for making all kinds of hanging decorations. If metal forms are used, soap them first, and cover any holes with masking tape to keep the plaster from seeping through. When plaster has been poured into the molds, add a looped piece of string for hanging, tying a knot at the open ends (Fig. 17-6A). These molds can be painted; leave the sharp white plaster showing as contrast to colors.

Fig. 17-6A: Seasonal hanging decorations
patterned from cooky cutters.

lesson 7

Printing Block for All Occasions

Procedure:

A good size block to handle can be made from a ½-pint cream carton, rinsed thoroughly. Pour the plaster, let set and dry, then remove the carton. Use the top surface to carve a design, such as a decorative bird (Fig. 17-7A). Since plaster is absorbent brush white shellac or varnish over the top, after the carving is finished. Use white linoleum block printing ink and dark or bright colored construction paper. Brush or roll ink over surface. Make a repeat design (Fig. 17-7B) for a good effect. See how many different ideas the pupils have. If letters are used, check back to lesson four to see how to reverse them, so the finished work will be correct.

Fig. 17-7A: Printing block.

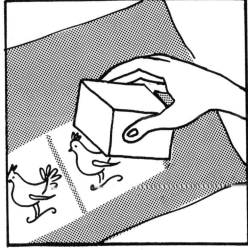

Fig. 17-7B: Making a repeat design with printing block.

lesson 8

Plaster of Paris Candle Base

Procedure:

Candles always add a festive look at holiday time, and extra handpainted ones will be welcome—especially if made by children. A double-tiered effect is made with foil baking cups. Use three cups together for added support when the plaster is poured into them. When the plaster begins to set, insert a wax candle in harmonious proportion to the base diameter. Make a second base; glue the one containing the candle on top. Paint with holiday colors and designs (Fig. 17-8A). These candle bases can be made for any holiday.

For a second style, use a larger cup but only fill it part way with plaster; fill a shallow plastic cover for a wider base; when dry glue the two together. The candle must be inserted as the plaster begins to set.

Fig. 17-8A: Centerpiece made of plaster
bases and wax candles.

lesson 9

Oval Cartoons and Wall Plaques

Procedure:

Line up several plastic picnic spoons of different sizes, resting them on a box so they will be level to hold the plaster without spilling over (Fig. 17-9A). Pour plaster into each spoon, let set and dry, then slip them out. Repeat until you have collected quite a few. This could be a two-lesson project: first the pouring, then the creative part—and these smooth oval shapes really challenge the imagination! Make a wall plaque of heavy paper onto which the ovals are glued to resemble a stem of pussywillows. Then paint in the stem and the black cups that hold the catkin. Try cartoons. See how many insects and animals or birds these ovals suggest to your pupils (Fig. 17-9B). Four ovals make a beautiful butterfly. The wings can be painted to resemble a particular insect. An ostrich is ideal—just add head, neck, plumes and legs. A turtle is easy. You will find yourself trying many other ideas with these plaster ovals.

Fig. 17-9A: Plastic picnic spoons make good molds.

Fig. 17-9B: Various uses for spoon-molded plaster shapes.

lesson 10

Large Plaster Beads

Procedure:

Mix the plaster of Paris but this time wait until it begins to harden; then spoon up a ball, rolling it between your hands (Fig. 17-10A). If it sticks a bit add a little plaster powder to your palms and continue to roll. A little water can be added if too dry. Spear these balls on a large knitting needle, being careful not to let them touch, and let them dry. Handpaint them while they are still on the knitting needle, and let them dry again. These can be sprayed with varnish or, easier in the classroom, they can be painted with Mod Podge, a milk solution that dries clear and makes an excellent finish.

Fig. 17-10A: Making jewelry from
plaster beads.

lesson 11

Painted Cartoon Display

Procedure:

This simple lesson provides such unusual display opportunities that it seems worthwhile to include it. Fill the sections of a TV dinner tray half full with plaster (Fig. 17-11A). Let it dry, then turn the tray upside down and bend the foil a bit to let the sections slip out. Place the sections on drawing paper and draw around them to find the size and shape each cartoon should be. Next, design original cartoons or copy your favorite ones and trace them onto the plaster shapes. Color them and outline them in black. Finally, glue the pieces to a sheet of cardboard for an attractive display (Fig. 17-11B).

Fig. 17-11A: Pouring plaster into TV dinner tray.

Fig. 17-11B: Painted cartoon display.

chapter eighteen

Creating Animals and Other Figures in Pariscraft

Introduction

Pariscraft is freely used in the classroom with enjoyable and successful results. This new modeling form is ideal for classrooms since it is a fabric, it is light in weight, it dries rapidly and it can be draped over live or inanimate objects, leaving detailed impressions. The potentials of art forms in Pariscraft are tremendous, ranging from simple projects to professional art objects. Pariscraft is a manufactured, pre-shrunk, non-toxic gauze saturated in plaster of Paris. Pariscraft for schools and organizations is purchased in 20-pound cartons containing rolls 2' to 6' in width and five yards long. It can also be purchased in local pharmacies where it is sold to make casts for broken bones. When you dip the stiff strips of Pariscraft in water, they become limp, dissolving the plaster to a creamy consistency and making it extremely workable, easy to drape over forms. When the gauze dries, it becomes lightweight, rigid as stone, and can be textured rough or smooth depending on the surface desired.

A white "sculpture" of Pariscraft looks very attractive, but your boys and girls may want to color figures such as birds and animals. You should have your class work on wax paper, since Pariscraft will stick to newspaper. Cut lengths of strips ahead of time. Keep strips away from water until you are ready to wet them; splashings will cause dry areas that will not reactivate. Be sure your pupils rinse and dry scissors immediately after using or they will rust. Do not tear Pariscraft—the dust can be injurious to some children and wastes the material. Protect sensitive hands with lotion.

lesson 1

How to Use Pariscraft

Procedure:

Don't let girls and boys begin working with Pariscraft without a pre-planned idea. Discuss plans; it will save time and material and prevent disappointment. Cut enough strips of Pariscraft the size you need—rather too many than not enough (Fig. 18-1A). Stack these strips so water will not splash on them. Dip the first strip in water gently. With the other hand guide off excess water into the bowl (Fig. 18-1B). Do not roughly squeeze the plaster out of the gauze, for it is an essential part of the medium. Drape the strips over the object you have chosen to work with, smoothing it out with your fingers, adding more water to make a creamy consistency. This is the basic process of Pariscraft; learn it thoroughly for efficiency, fun and success.

Fig. 18-1A: Cutting strips of Pariscraft.

Fig. 18-1B: Dipping the strips in water.

lesson 2

Pariscraft over an Armature

Procedure:

An armature is a framework of metal used by a sculptor to model clay over a skeleton. In this case, instead of wire, four pipe cleaners 6″ long make the armature. Bend three of these in half (in ''U'' shapes) for arms, legs and body; shape the fourth into a circle for the head (Fig. 18-2A). Complete the figure by joining these sections. Drip the gauze strips in water, then wrap them around the figure until it is completely covered, forming hands and feet as you work. Let the figure dry on wax paper, bending it into an action pose (Fig. 18-2B). Display these figures mounted on bright blue construction paper. They will be easy to glue since the back of the figure, having dried on the wax paper, will be flat.

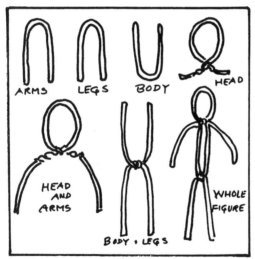

Fig. 18-2A: Pipe cleaner armature for figures.

Fig. 18-2B: Armature covered with Pariscraft.

lesson 3

Action Figures
Without Armatures

Procedure:

Students are often so interested in making action figures that you may want to offer another simple lesson, using only a small amount of Pariscraft. Measure out two dry strips, one long enough to form arms and head, and the other one the right length to form the body and legs (Fig. 18-3A). Dip one strip in water and twist with both hands, smoothing out any frayed edges. Place this strip on wax paper and shape into hands, arms and head. Twist the second strip into legs and body, and join to the first strip. Then bend the figure into a distinctive pose and let it dry. Dancing or sports poses are effective. When the figure dries it will be stiff, and you can lean it against a wall or hang it up. Since the figure rests on wax paper as it dries the back will be flat, so it can be easily mounted on a background, which can be a solid color or painted to indicate a specific theme. The figure should be left white (Fig. 18-3B).

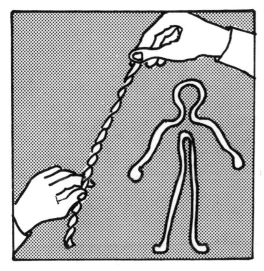

Fig. 18-3A: Figure made with twisted strip.

Fig. 18-3B: Figures showing action.

lesson 4

Figure Built over
a Plastic Container

Procedure:

A small plastic container, such as those used for cleansing powder and shaped like a human form, is excellent as a base for a figure. When empty, fill it with sand to weigh it down, then cover with Pariscraft, make circular arms and attach to body, leaving space to hold pencils. Cover a small plastic lid with the material for the base; create a cartoon head and attach it to the body. This would make an amusing gift (Fig. 18-4A).

Fig. 18-4A: Figure from a plastic container.

lesson 5

Hand Puppet in Two Sections

Procedure:

Cut a stack of strips measuring 1″ wide to about 6″ long; keep away from water. Pupils can work in pairs with this project: however, it can also be a one-person project, depending on the age level. Keep the fingers closed; dip strips in water and wrap them around the fingers—making them just loose enough to permit fingers to bend. Do two or three layers. After a few minutes the Pariscraft will begin to harden, making it possible to wiggle the fingers and slip off the "cast." Place it on the wax paper to dry flat. Repeat the same process, wrapping strips dipped in water around the lower part of the hand. Do not wrap around the wrist but rather extend the hand width down evenly. After

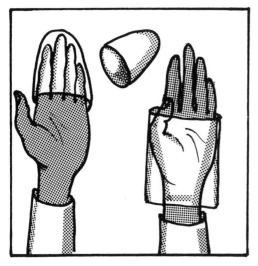

Fig. 18-5A: Hand puppet—first step.

Fig. 18-5B: Hand puppet—second step.

Fig. 18-5C: Hand puppet—completed.

a few minutes when the Pariscraft begins to set, remove it and let it dry. (Fig. 18-5A). Cut a strip of white sheeting 3″ wide and long enough to go around the cast. Glue it in place, separating the two casts by about 2½″ and allowing a full ½″ for overlapping the casts to permit the hand to bend. Let it dry thoroughly. Paint with paint or markers a bright red open mouth and two cartoon eyes. Attach black yarn hair (Fig. 18-5B). Manipulate the hand puppet by inserting the hand and bending the head forward, closing and opening the mouth. When the puppet is not in use place it standing up, with the head, which is slightly smaller, resting inside the lower section—and the wrinkles will make an amusing expression (Fig. 18-5C).

lesson 6

Small Solid Figures

Procedure:

Using a duck for an example, make a drawing of him, keeping it small for practice in this particular animation (Fig. 18-6A). Draw a dotted line on the neck where it is to be separated; curl a short wire (aluminum utility) over and around a pencil to make a short spiral shape; set it aside. With small pieces of Pariscraft make head, beak, two webbed feet, and two wings separately. Form the body of the duck, insert the coiled wire in body and head, and squeeze

Fig. 18-6A: Making a solid Pariscraft figure.

Fig. 18-6B: Small movable figures.

material firmly around wire to make it secure (Fig. 18-6B). When dry stand him up and check balance. Try other animated cartoon figures; dogs are easy to make. The small movable figures make amusing gifts.

lesson 7

Horse Head Bookends

Procedure:

An excellent, useful, heavy bookend is made by draping Pariscraft over two matched rocks, basically alike in size and shape. Start by cutting a few Pariscraft squares large enough to cover the rocks. Dip the squares in water and cover the rocks completely—top, sides, and bottom. After the rocks are covered, begin to build out the profile of a horse's head. Two sketches would be helpful—one front view, same size as the Pariscraft bookend, and the other a clear profile. These bookends are most effective if left white (Fig. 18-7A). Glue a piece of felt on the base to prevent marking table surface.

Fig. 18-7A: Horse head bookends.

lesson 8

"Pop Art" Sculpture

Procedure:

The human hand makes an excellent model, either for "Pop Art" sculpture or for an unusual dish. An older student could make this by himself, but it is more successful when done by two. If the model has sensitive skin, cover his hand with lotion and let dry. Apply strips of Pariscraft over the top of the hand after the desired position has been decided upon (Fig. 18-8A). Keep pressing into the shape of the hand to get the imprint of muscles and bone structure for a realistic effect. After the top begins to dry it will be possible to wiggle the fingers away from the cast, leaving it shaped like the hand. Remove, let dry, and—holding the model's hand in the same pose—repeat the process for the other half of the hand. When this second section has dried, use short pieces of Pariscraft to fasten the two sections together. The open end can be filled in or left open. The plaster hand can be used as a candy dish or stood upright as "Pop Art" sculpture, a definite conversation piece (Fig. 18-8B).

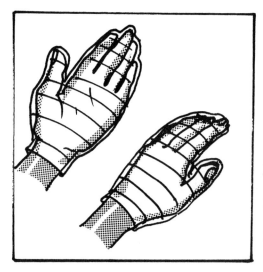

Fig. 18-8A: Hand used as model for "Pop Art."

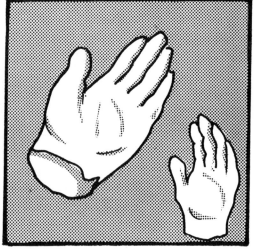

Fig. 18-8B: Completed "Pop Art."

lesson 9

Pinocchio Finger Puppet (Changeable Head)

Procedure:

Here is an inexpensive way for pupils to make their own hand puppets to use in acting out different stories in the classroom and at home. Since the story of Pinocchio involves the changing length of his nose, three heads should be made—one with a normal nose, one with a noticeably longer nose, and one with a very long nose. Wrap Pariscraft around the index finger so it fits—but not too tightly. Make a head including a neck to hide the finger. Make a little hat by folding some Pariscraft into a pointed top and adding a brim. Make three heads all the same size, then attach the three noses—one on each head (Fig. 18-9A). Make two hands to fit over the thumb and middle finger, flaring out the edge of the Pariscraft so the costume can be sewn or tied onto it. As the play progresses, the heads change, until finally in the last scene Pinocchio is back to normal.

Fig. 18-9A: Changeable heads for
Pinocchio puppet.

lesson 10

Self-Portrait
on Newspaper Armature

Procedure:

First construct a post in a base, which can be made in different ways. One suggestion is to embed a short thick branch in plaster of Paris poured into a box, let it set, wrap newspaper tightly around the post, forming a head-shaped mass, then tie it with string. This inner structure saves on the Pariscraft material. Begin to build Pariscraft over the armature, shaping a head of yourself or of a famous person. Use two pictures for reference, for front and side views. Make the head bald at first and then add the hair. Bangs and upturned hair can be dried on hair curlers. (See Fig. 18-10A).

Fig. 18-10A: Self-portrait made on
newspaper armatures.

lesson 11

Three-String Marionette

Procedure:

A good way to introduce the art of manipulating a marionette is to start with a three-string puppet. Make the body and legs of one piece; make a head and two arms. Again the way to save on Pariscraft is to make tight wads of newspaper tied with string for the inside, then wrap the wads with Pariscraft. Make three joints (of either pipe cleaners or wire) by making one loop, twisting the ends closed, and threading a second wire through, looping and closing. When the body, arms and legs are ready, insert the joints, adding small pieces of Pariscraft to hold the wires firmly in the Pariscraft. A single loop is used for the top of the head. Cut three strings the length needed for the table height and ease in handling; then loop the three ends, slip onto the fingers, and the marionette is ready for action (Fig. 18-11A).

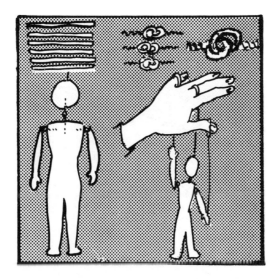

Fig. 18-11A: A Pariscraft marionette.

lesson 12

All-White Seasonal Ornaments

Procedure:

Pariscraft is perfect for ornaments and decorations because it dries quickly, is light in weight and delightful to paint on, especially since its clean white background sets off color so well. There are two ways to make a little "cage" for holding ornaments (Fig. 18-12A). The first way is to use a large balloon, and, working with another pupil, stretch the balloon and insert seasonal objects, such as small Christmas tree balls. Blow the balloon up to the desired size. Stretch strips of Pariscraft (cut ahead of time and dipped in water) around the balloon. Let dry thoroughly, then prick the rubber and watch the balloon collapse, revealing a cage with colored items inside.

A "cage" made of a small paper cup makes a good table favor, or a hanging tiny basket. Simply cover a cup smoothly with Pariscraft, let it dry, then slip out the mold. This results in a delightful little basket, which can be painted. Another unusual hanging ornament, which can be decorated for any season, uses a larger cup, upside down. Drape strips of Pariscraft around it in a spiral design, covering the base and adding at least four vertical strips to support the spiral when it is dry. Slip the cup out, pierce the top with a small hole to thread a string through, and attach some seasonal ornament to hang within the spiral form.

Fig. 18-12A: All-white all-seasonal ornaments.

lesson 13

Life-Size "Pop" Sculpture

Recently a group of high school students were inspired by the work of George Segal, a noted American sculptor, to create some very striking figures. As described in the *McGraw-Hill Dictionary of Art* (Vol. 5, p. 141), Mr. Segal ". . . created entire scenes in which figures are produced by taking plaster casts of living people and placing them in settings such as gas stations, diners, and buses. The anonymous white figures, with their features smoothed over, are pictorially united by the physical and emotional consistency of enervation and isolation."

The students experimented with this technique, dipping gauze into plaster and covering live models with it, with attractive results. You may want to undertake a similar project with your older pupils, taking all necessary precautions. In this case, the students first explored the Pariscraft medium, then they thoroughly planned the work with artists and models, deciding on themes before any work began. Working in groups, they decided to illustrate restful moments in student lives. The heads were cast at home under parent supervision, so casting could be stopped immediately if any model experienced trouble with sensitive skin or allergies to the Pariscraft.

Each head is started by fitting foil closely over the face, with air holes at the nostrils. Pariscraft strips are applied to the foil, constantly and gently pressed down to develop the contour of the bone structure of the face underneath. The front and the back of the head are done separately (Fig. 18-13A).

The Pariscraft will dry in a short time; when it does, remove the mask. Do not add eyebrows, but leave the mask as it is. Some students added the ear with the front half of the face; others made a separate ear and secured in place when head was completed. Next cover the head with a bathing cap and make the back of the head; when dry join it to the front with strips of gauze dipped in water. Finally make the hair. If the hair was turned up or had bangs that fluffed out, simply shape it over hair curlers for a few minutes (Fig. 18-13B), slip it off, and the hair looks realistic. Clothes were worn that had no nap; materials like heavy denims were excellent as the Pariscraft fitted well over the wrinkles and shapes, and dried and slipped off easily. The high school students made three life-size figures modelled directly over their clothes. The results were fascinating, with each one easily recognizable. To try a more difficult pose, one of the boys had the idea of being cast sitting on a tall stool, holding his fishing pole (Fig. 18-13C), which he brought in when the display was set up in the large showcase in the school foyer. Another model was holding a candy bar and soft drink bottle; the third was resting against a wall holding flowers, with a basket nearby filled with artificial blooms. Overhead lighting gave a dramatic effect to the whole scene.

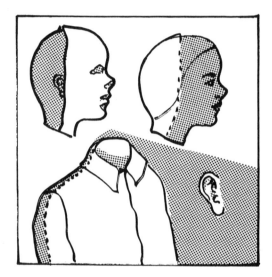

Fig. 18-13A: Molding life-size "Pop" sculpture.

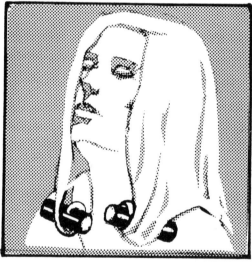

Fig. 18-13B: Completed model of head, showing hair curlers.

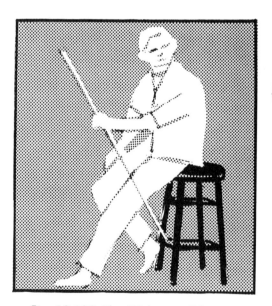

Fig. 18-13C: The "Fisherman" figure.

Glossary

Abstract ... not easily understood.

Accordion fold ... a method of folding paper (or other material) in forward and backward bends to form pleats like those in an accordion.

Acrylic paint ... (also called Polymer); a plastic paint scientifically manufactured, which dries hard and will not fade.

Analogous colors ... neighboring colors on the color wheel: for example, yellow, yellow green, green, green blue, blue, etc.

Armature ... the framework for supporting the material (plaster, clay, Pariscraft, etc.) used in modeling figures and animals.

Bamboo brush ... a brush made with a bamboo handle, desirable because of its lightness.

Batik ... a method of dyeing in which parts of a fabric are coated with removable wax so that part of the fabric will not receive the dye.

Central balance ... an essential feature of any design that grows from the center out in orderly fashion.

Chinese brushwork ... painting that follows Oriental tradition, involving full control of a special brush (usually bamboo).

Collage ... a design or picture composed of either a single or multiple materials glued to a surface in realistic, conventional or abstract theme.

Color perspective ... achieving a sense of distance in perspective through the gradual dimming of colors.

Conté crayon ... a crayon made of a mixture of graphite and clay, invented by Nicolas Jacques Conté (1755–1805), a French artist who was skilled in the manufacture of materials.

Cool colors ... in color perspective, these colors recede: green, blue, purple.
Contour ... the outline of a figure or object.

Counterchange ... to transpose, or interchange; here used specifically in the sense of transposing two colors, or black and white.

Cray-Pas ... a soft crayon made by combining crayon and pastel.

Cubism ... an art form characterized by the use of cubes and other geometric forms in abstract arrangements.

Dry brush ... a technique in which a paint brush is dragged across the paper releasing paint until just enough pigment is left to create a series of fine hairlines, ideal for suggesting grass, bark and hair.

Emboss ... to decorate or cover with designs, patterns, etc. raised above the surface.

Encaustic ... a method of painting in which crayon tips, touched to a candle flame, are applied immediately to a drawing while in the melting stage.

Etching with crayon ... a method of producing a design by cutting through layers of crayon with a sharp implement.

Expressionism ... any form of art characterized by distortion of reality to give objective expression to inner experience.

Fabric crayons ... crayons which, when applied to cloth or paper and pressed with a hot iron, become permanent.

Fingerpaint ... a heavy, creamy paint created by Mildred Shaw, which is spread over the paper by using the fingers or hand.

Fingerpaint paper ... a non-absorbent glossy paper used especially for fingerpaint.

Flat papier mache ... art medium made of layers of newspaper pasted together and smoothed out flat and even, and while damp shaped into forms.

Freebrush ... painting directly and freely on the paper, using no outlines.

Frozen hand ... the technique of holding the fingers in a "frozen" pose, essential to clear, strong fingerpaint pictures.

Geometric forms ... basic shapes, used in two or three dimensions: square, oval, circle, triangle, cylinder.

Gouache ... a way of painting with opaque colors ground in water and mixed with a preparation of gum.

Half-pans ... small metal or plastic containers for watercolor in dry cake form; found in watercolor sets of 8 or 16 colors.

Impasto ... paint laid thickly on the paper or canvas.

Impressionism ... a school of painting that emphasizes the capturing of a momentary glimpse of a subject and the reproduction of the changing effects of light through short strokes of pure color.

Isolation pictures ... made by using block-out material such as rubber cement, tape, Maskoid, on areas to be left white, then washing over picture with color and removing block-out when dry.

Japanese rice paper ... a fine, delicate paper, transparent and textured with fibers; ideal for Chinese brushwork.

Kinetic art ... an art style involving the use of moving parts.

Laminated ... composed of or built in thin sheets or layers, as of fabric, wood, plastic, etc. that have been bonded or pressed together; often used in transparent projects.

Maraca ... a percussion instrument consisting of a dried gourd or a gourd-shaped rattle filled with pebbles; Brazilian in origin.

Marionette ... a puppet or little jointed doll moved by strings or wire from above, frequently manipulated by moving a wooden bar to which the strings are attached.

Maskoid and Miskit ... block-out liquids used to prevent color from touching the paper; when paint is dry, these materials can be rubbed off, leaving clean white paper.

Matte knife ... an art knife with a changeable double-edged blade.

Medium ... the material the artist is working in: pencil, crayon, ink, etc.; plural, *media*.

Metal ferrule ... the metal band that encloses the hair in a paintbrush and fastens it to the handle.

Mildred Shaw ... the inventor of fingerpainting.

Mixed media ... refers to the use of more than one material in a single painting.

Mobiles ... abstract constructions, balanced and suspended in midair and set in motion by air currents.

Mod Podge ... a milky white liquid which, when applied to a drawing, dries clear and forms a protective varnish.

Monochromatic painting ... painting done in one color, to which white or black can be added for lighter or darker tints.

Monograms ... personal initials pleasingly designed, either inside or outside a border.

Montage ... a pictorial composition consisting of one or many photographs or pictures.

Motivate ... to inspire the pupils with enthusiasm for a lesson.

Mystic Tape ... strong tape, plastic on one side, which comes in various colors and widths.

Mural ... a decorative picture painted on a wall or fastened to a wall surface.

Negative space ... space between objects in a picture.

Non-absorbent palette ... a palette made of any material that does not absorb: foil, glass, metal, enamel, wax paper, parchment; especially important for use with acrylic paint.

Oaktag ... a smooth, hard-surface, lightweight cardboard.

"Op art" ... (short for optical art), a style of abstract painting utilizing geometrical patterns or figures to create various optical effects, such as the illusion of movement. (Note: "Op art" is not used in the text but the terms "pop art" and "op art" are often used together, so it is included here.

Painting knife ... an extremely flexible knife with a wafer-thin tempered steel blade and a bent handle for easy grip.

Pariscraft ... a pre-shrunk gauze saturated with plaster of Paris, which, when wet, becomes limp for modeling over objects; dries hard.

Payons ... painting crayons so manufactured that when water is applied to the crayon drawing it immediately bleeds color.

Pictorial collage ... a collage made by pasting various materials onto a background to form a picture.

Plaque ... a thin, flat plate or piece of wood, decorated and hung on a wall for ornamentation.

Plaster of Paris ... a heavy white powder, calcined gypsum, which, when mixed with water, forms a thick paste that sets quickly; used for casts, molds, etc.

Plasticine ... a non-hardening oil base modeling clay.

Pointillism ... the method of painting that uses tiny dots of pure color that blend together when seen from a distance, producing a luminous effect.

"Pop art" ... (short for popular art), a realistic art style, especially in painting and sculpture, using techniques and popular subjects adapted from commercial art and the mass communications media, such as comic strips, posters, etc.

Positive space ... space that represents the subject of the painting itself.

Reverse etching ... a process in which paper is depressed by pressing lines into it without breaking through it, and then rubbing over the paper with a crayon, leaving white lines in the depressed areas.

Rubber cement ... a waterproof glue.

Rubbing ... the art of revealing designs by placing a paper on top of a surface bearing a raised or cut-in pattern and rubbing with the flat side of a crayon.

Sgraffito ... a method of producing a design by scratching away the outer coating.

Silhouette ... an outline drawing filled in, usually with black ink; named after Etienne de Silhouette (1709–1767), who created amateur portraits by this method.

Slab sculpture ... sculpture made by pasting together a number of shapes made of papier mache.

Spatter ... tapping the brush on the edge of a ruler so as to cause large and small spots of paint to fall onto the painting.

Stained glass transparencies ... pictures created on white paper which has been colored and oiled, causing a transparent effect.

Stencil ... a thin sheet of paper or other material perforated in such a way that color rubbed over it will form a design on the material underneath.

Stippling ... applying paint in small points or dots rather than in lines or solid areas.

Sumi ... (Japanese); black sticks of carbon mixed with glue; these sticks are ground in water to create the ink used for drawing.

Tempera ... an opaque, water-base paint—the direct opposite of watercolor.

Textures in watercolor ... changes in the appearance of the paper, achieved by using art tools to create the semblance of fur, bark, wood grain, etc.

Three-dimensional ... appearing to have depth or thickness in addition to height and width.

Warm colors ... in color perspective, these colors advance: red, yellow, orange.

Wash-away crayon ... a special crayon which, when directly applied to plastic for instruction purposes, can be washed off or left on for final drawing.

Watercolor ... a pigment or coloring matter that is mixed with water for use as a paint; watercolor technique is to use more water than color.

Watercolor crayons ... water-soluble crayons.

Wax paper etching ... an etching produced by rubbing Cray-Pas over wax paper and cutting through it to reveal white lines.

Wet-in-wet ... a painting technique in which a second color is painted directly into a wet surface.

Index